# Critical Issues in Educational Leadership Series
## Joseph Murphy, Series Editor

# SCHOOLS
# FOR
# SALE

*Why Free Market Policies
Won't Improve America's Schools,
and What Will*

### ERNEST R. HOUSE

**TEACHERS
COLLEGE
♔PRESS**

Teachers College, Columbia University
New York and London

Published by Teachers College Press, 1234 Amsterdam Avenue, New York, NY 10027

*Library of Congress Cataloging-in-Publication Data*
House, Ernest R.
    Schools for sale : why free market policies won't improve America's schools, and what will /
Ernest R. House.
        p.    cm.
    Includes bibliographical references (p.    ) and index.
    ISBN 0-8077-3738-0 (cloth). — ISBN 0-8077-3737-2 (pbk.)
        1. Education—Economic aspects—United States.    2. Education and state—United States.
    3. School improvement programs—United States.    4. Educational vouchers—United States.
    I. Title.
    LC66.H68    1998
    379.73—dc21                                                                                                97-46820

ISBN 0-8077-3737-2 (paper)
ISBN 0-8077-3738-0 (cloth)

Printed on acid-free paper

Manufactured in the United States of America

05    04    03    02    01    00    99    98        8    7    6    5    4    3    2    1

# CONTENTS

*For Paul, whose spirit and endurance have amazed us all*

# POLICIES, MARKETS, AND TEACHER ASSETS

Over the past 30 years, one of the most persistent features of educational life has been that innovations are advanced, have brief lives, then disappear, without affecting the schools in any significant way. There are exceptions to this trend, but not many. In fact, the schools look pretty much the same now as they did decades ago. Why is this? Why have the schools been so slow to change in significant ways? After all, thousands of people have invested incredible amounts of energy to transform them.

This book attempts to answer that question, based on my years of dealing with educational change as an evaluator and policy analyst. My explanation, expounded in this book, runs along these lines. Those who make policies for the schools—politicians, bureaucrats, business leaders—formulate educational policy with a view to general economic development, or what they think will result in improved economic prospects. Such behavior is reasonable since most politicians stay in office because of good economic conditions or lose office plagued by bad ones. Their political survival depends on economic prosperity.

The problem is that in formulating these educational policies, policymakers do not take sufficient account of how the schools actually function, or the kinds of people that teachers and educators are. That is to say, teachers and educators are much like everyone else. The types of policies proposed for schools would rarely be proposed for business enterprises because policymakers have a more realistic view of how businesses operate. One can hardly imagine the president formulating national goals for American business and expecting businesses to follow the goals simply because the president enunciated them. Yet such is the case for American education. Hence, the educational policies proposed usually fail in what they intend.

Furthermore, it is clear when these policies are announced that they are likely to fail, at least to those who understand schools. But these people have little say about the policies, except as critics, and their criticisms are interpreted as resistance to change and dismissed accordingly. So we are launched into failure after failure. It is no wonder that teachers become cynical about educational reforms, refuse to cooperate, or participate without commitment.

In this book I address this problem in two ways. First, I examine the relationships between educational policies and economic conditions and review the educational policies of the Reagan–Bush and Clinton administrations. I judge most of these educational policies to be unlikely to succeed. I also question common assumptions about the relationship between education and economic productivity. Attempts to make the schools more productive often make them less so.

Second, and more importantly, I present an appraisal framework whereby one can determine whether an educational policy is likely to succeed or fail before it is implemented. I call the framework presented in the second half of the book an appraisal framework rather than an evaluation one in the sense that a jeweler can appraise a diamond, that is, determine its potential value. From this framework one can ask, does this new policy meet these basic criteria for success? Does it have a chance? Conducting such an appraisal would save much effort and grief.

This appraisal framework is adapted from microeconomic theory, specifically from a recently developed branch called transaction cost economics. The theory treats human transactions in the economic realm as contractual relationships and poses questions as to what conditions are necessary for such contracts to succeed. Although this doesn't sound immediately promising as an approach to understanding educational change, the theory provides insights not available from other sources and identifies educational policies unlikely to succeed. The framework highlights the weaknesses that these policies possess.

When one treats educational change as a contractual relationship between innovators and teachers, teachers are regarded as full partners in the enterprise, partners whose cooperation is necessary to make any significant change. Teachers are seen not as compliant functionaries or selfless saints, but rather as people who must pay some significant costs for educational change to occur and who will want something back for their efforts. In other words, they are pretty much like anyone else in any enterprise. Change cannot be cost free, according to transaction cost economics. The issues then are what the costs will be, how costs can be minimized, who will bear them, and how they can be managed.

The three key attributes common to parties in contractual relationships are bounded rationality, opportunism, and the holding of specific assets. Parties cannot be expected to know everything or foresee everything. They cannot be expected to be totally free of opportunistic motivations, whether opportunism is manifested in pursuing subgoals not covered by the agreement or their own interests. And over time participants may be expected to develop assets specific to the situation in which they work. That is to say, both teachers and students develop knowledge and skills specific to each other, their peers, and the specific context. One might consider such knowledge and skills as assets, assets born of investing in learning on the job. Often these assets are overlooked or underappreciated.

As with a knowing departmental secretary who has been around for 20 years, such knowledge may be invaluable, though totally specific to the department. Specific assets are not easily transferable. Knowledge of people and procedures in the old department may not apply in a new one. Nonetheless, these assets are valuable, and the holder of them might be expected to resist their diminution or even sharing them with others, as with any valuable assets.

Transactions involving specific assets operate differently from those without. Markets involving specific assets do not operate like the impersonal markets of neoclassical theory. The development of specific assets by teachers and students has important implications for educational policies, especially those involving educational choice and markets, since often these policies do not consider teacher assets, or student ones either, for that matter.

Most reforms fail on some or all these criteria. They assume that teachers know how to achieve things they do not, or that they are selfless and will do what they are told, or that they do not possess knowledge and skills laboriously acquired, which they are loath to abandon despite admonitions to move on to other modes of teaching. Some reforms assume that new knowledge of how to do things is readily available when it is not. On the other hand, there are reforms that do take account of such key attributes, successful reforms like Central Park East, reforms that build on the assets of teachers and students. For successful reform to be possible, one must have a realistic grasp of schools and teachers, including recognition of teacher assets.

In the final analysis, improving productivity in the schools depends on understanding the transactions that take place in them before one can substitute better forms of instruction. I believe that significant productivity advances are possible by basic transformations in the school's operations, so that classrooms will look and function differently from the way they do now. I suggest ways in which classrooms can be organized to take advantage of teachers as tutors and discussion leaders, rather than as information presenters. But before we arrive at such transformed schools we need to recognize how to get there, what kinds of exchanges and resources are necessary, what costs must be incurred. After all, no transformation of any major enterprise was ever cost free.

This book is divided into two parts. Part I, "Big Policy," discusses the relationships between educational policy and national economic concerns, as applied to developed countries. It critiques American educational policies over the past 20 years and questions assumptions about the connections between education and economic progress. Part II, "Little Policy," presents the appraisal framework, adapted from transaction cost economics, and applies this framework to many current educational reform proposals, from national standards to school vouchers to Central Park East. The book concludes with a reflection on how economic concepts pervade all aspects of our lives. Where are we going?

# BIG POLICY

Part I of this book deals with three education-economy relationships: how economic policies and conditions affect educational policy; how education is involved in the economy at a macro-level; and how economic and business concepts and metaphors penetrate government policy. Chapter 1 is an analysis of the influence of economic thinking on educational policy, followed by an overview of education policies in the United States in the 1980s. Reagan–Bush education policies were formulated with a view to addressing the consequences of far-reaching and sometimes socially disruptive economic policies, policies that increased income inequality. In brief, education was scapegoated for social disruption and failed economic policies, a blame most educators accepted willingly. Students were seen as not only uneducated but also undisciplined, which called for coercive correction.

The next chapter focuses on Clinton's education policies, especially national standards, national testing, and systemic change. On taking office Clinton was faced with severe budget problems from previous administrations, so his educational policies had to cost little new money and not threaten the middle classes, who felt squeezed in the new global economy. These policies have little chance of changing the schools in any effective way since they are based on faulty assumptions. The policies either call for reforms of state governments or would cost large sums of money for teacher retraining.

The fourth chapter is a discussion of education's relationship to the economy. The dominant neoconservative and neoliberal views of how education and the economy fit together are challenged by a more complex perspective in line with the thinking of human capital theorists. The productivity problem of the American economy started with business enterprises, not in education. It is not only that education creates jobs, but also that jobs create education. People will undertake education when they see a payoff. If good jobs are not there, then education will suffer. It is an open question whether it is in the interest of global corporations to support expensive education systems in their home country if they can find educated workers elsewhere.

The fifth chapter is a slight detour in the main argument of how to improve education. It deals with the penetration of government by business concepts. With Clinton's "reinventing government" reform, the government was to be manager, rather than producer, of government services. Services could be better produced by private enterprises under government guidance. An ambitious agenda was introduced to reform the federal bureaucracy. These reforms have had limited success. The general problem of applying business concepts to government, such as contracting out government services, is analyzed in detail, using the outsourcing of evaluation services as an example.

Part II deals with how to improve educational productivity at the school level, the micro-level where the actual educational work takes place.

# CHAPTER 1

# POLICY AND PRODUCTIVITY IN EDUCATION

*Indeed, as we now see with painful clearness, we have, in the long run, for the maintenance of our pre-eminent industrial position in the world, nothing to depend on except the brains of our people. Public education has, therefore, insensibly come to be regarded not as a matter of philanthropy undertaken for the sake of the individual children benefited, but as a matter of national concern undertaken in the interest of the community as a whole.*

—(Webb, 1904, quoted in Vaizey, 1962, p. 9)

*We are slowly beginning to see, as well, that the great battles of the world in the future are to be commercial rather than military or naval, and that it is our duty to get ready for them if we wish to prosper as a nation. The trained artisan is to be the private; the trained leader the captain; and an educated, sober, capable, and industrious people the base of supplies for the national armies of the future. Whether we like it or not, we are beginning to see that we are pitted against the world in a gigantic battle of brains and skill, with the markets of the world, work for our people, and internal peace and contentment as the prizes at stake.*

—(Cubberley, 1909, pp. 49–50)

We live in an age of economic productivity, during a time in which the dominant concerns in many countries are expanding the economy, raising personal income, and increasing the standard of living. No government in liberal democracies can long survive without economic expansion, whether the country is run by conservatives, social democrats, or socialists (or apparently communists either). This concern for productivity is manifested in a drive for greater efficiency and has special implications for education. In fact, it is the source of most educational policy at the national and state levels. Educational productivity I take to mean increasing the learning of students significantly or doing the same job with the same effectiveness for less money.

Although productivity is a central concern in all industrial countries, it results in somewhat different educational policies in each. Britain, the oldest industrial economy, is different from the mature economy of the United States, which is

7

different again from the economies of Japan and Germany, or the young economy of Spain, or the resource-based economy of Australia. One national educational system expands even while another contracts painfully. Nonetheless, in most countries national educational policies appear to be formulated primarily with regard to the national economy and without sufficient regard for educational practice.

By policies, I mean those ideas, concepts, programs, and laws endorsed by the top policymakers in the country or state that lead the government in certain directions. Policymakers certainly include the president or prime minister, cabinet officers, senior bureaucrats, and key legislators, as well as leaders of powerful interest groups, like the National Association of Governors, the Council of Chief State School Officers, and other national organizations. At the state level education policymakers include governors or premiers, their staffs, key state legislators, state boards of education, and, again, interest groups. Powerful business groups are involved at all levels.

Of course, other factors, like culture and history, influence educational policies as well. For example, racial politics permeates everything in America and is not duplicated elsewhere, though some countries show signs of catching up. Britain clings to its eternal class structure, which manifests itself throughout British life. Spain nurtures a virile traditionalism that suffuses both its life-style and bureaucracies, while Australia has its egalitarian "tall poppy" syndrome. Nonetheless, in spite of these differences, in all these countries economic concerns influence educational policy more strongly than anything else at the current time (Boyd & Kerchner, 1988; Wirt & Harmon, 1986).

I am *not* saying that economic policies necessarily influence educational *practices*. Educational practices (everyday teaching and learning patterns of teachers, students, and administrators) have many influences other than government policies; in fact, practices frequently run counter to policies. Furthermore, policies have effects opposite to what is intended. I am not advancing a functionalist explanation of educational change in which education and work mirror each other (a contested topic in the neo-Marxist literature, e.g., Apple & Weiss, 1983; Bowles & Gintis, 1976; Carnoy & Levin, 1985; Liston, 1988). Nor am I proposing that policies and practices mirror each other faithfully. They do not.

Rather, my contention is that national and state leaders formulate educational policies primarily in response to national or state economic concerns— without sufficient understanding or appreciation of educational institutions. This overdrawn focus causes educational policies to be mismatched to practices. Policies intended to increase productivity may decrease it. It's as if suggestions for improving productivity in the automobile industry were made without detailed knowledge of how cars are assembled. In Sarason's (1990) words, "those outside the system have nothing resembling a holistic conception of the system they seek to influence. In principle . . . ignorance need not be lethal, although it almost always has been" (p. 27).

Nor do government leaders do this deliberately with foreknowledge that their policies will fail. Rather they are mistaken in their initiatives because they are too far removed from contact with educational work, too wedded to powerful interests, too imbued with misleading ideologies, and simply misinformed. Thus, educational policies dissolve into ineffectiveness, to be replaced by other mistaken and ineffective policies. My analysis is an "error theory" of policy that explains why we have the policies we do and why these policies fail, to be replaced by other policies that also fail.

## WHY PRODUCTIVITY?

In recent years the open window of opportunity in American education policy has been productivity, a key economic concept. Economists play influential roles in domestic and foreign policy, raising questions such as "How does this policy increase productivity?" or "Can productivity be improved?" Economic productivity—increased production for the same or less cost—is closely tied to the standard of living. Heightened concern for productivity is integral to advanced capitalism. Unless productivity improves, one group's standard of living improves at another's expense. Economic concepts shape all aspects of social life. As a political economist has noted:

> Yet another characteristic of a market economy is a tendency to incorporate every aspect of society into the nexus of market relations. Through such "commercialization," the market generally brings all facets of society into the orbit of the price mechanism. Land, labor, and other so-called factors of production become commodities to be exchanged; they are subject to the interplay of market forces. . . . Stated more crudely, everything has its price and, as an economist friend is fond of saying, "Its value is its price." As a consequence, markets have a profound and destabilizing impact on society because they dissolve traditional structures and social relations. (Gilpin, 1987, p. 20)

One can add education to the factors of production in the modern economy. Put another way, the deterioration of traditional social institutions—family, community, and church—has led to social disarray, thus increasing the urgency of providing the population with even more material benefits. The legitimacy of the government itself rests on improving the material well-being of its citizens. In fact, governments cannot survive without doing so. As market relations destroy communal and traditional bases of support, the government must rely on material means of securing compliance. This means government becoming more dependent on business enterprises, which produce the wealth in capitalist societies. A British anthropologist has put the situation even more bluntly:

> Industrial society is the only society ever to live by and rely on sustained and perpetual growth, on an expected and continuous improvement. Not surprisingly, it was the first society to invent the concept and idea of progress, of continuous improvement. Its favoured mode of social control is universal Danegeld, buying off social aggression with material enhancement; its greatest weakness is its inability to survive any temporary reduction of the social bribery fund, and to weather the loss of legitimacy which befalls it if the cornucopia becomes temporarily jammed and the flow falters. (Gellner, 1983, p. 22)

The modern state and its politicians find themselves caught in the vise of the markets, often portrayed as representing natural law, but in any case apparently the only way to produce wealth for societies that increasingly depend on their material productivity, even as the markets disrupt other aspects of social life, which in turn undermines the legitimacy of the government—not an easy situation for governments to be in.

> If we ask what is the immediate central political issue in capitalism—the issue that takes on an often obsessive prominence in every capitalist nation—there is no question where to look. It is the relationship between business and government, or from our more distant perspective, between the economy and the state. (Heilbroner, 1993, p. 68)

Frequently, policies dedicated to efficiency and productivity in education do not result in better education or improved productivity. A series of educational failures litters the reform path. Nonetheless, misguided policies continue to be advanced and to secure high-level support.


## THE INFLUENCE OF ECONOMICS

There are at least four ways in which economic concerns influence educational policies. First, economic conditions strongly influence educational policies. For example, national and state budgets constrain educational spending. The expansionist policies of the 1950s and 1960s cannot be repeated in the 1990s, even if policymakers wanted to, because the budget surpluses are not there. Furthermore, economic policies have far-reaching consequences, such as increasing income inequality or increasing immigration, that the schools must contend with. They must deal with the poor and non-native speakers.

Second, educational policies are frequently formulated to reduce costs and increase the productivity of schools. This pressure is more than a budget consideration. The market forces of advanced capitalism work to increase the efficiency and productivity of all institutions, as they have done in agriculture and automobile manufacture. It may well be education's turn for economic rationalization.

At other times considerations such as defense, or caring for the disabled, or the assimilation of immigrants prevailed.

Third, education and economic development are presumed to be closely linked. It is assumed that more or better education leads to improved technological capabilities and better jobs. This connection is taken for granted for the most part and provides the rationale for much educational policy proposed by educators and noneducators, though this relationship is less straightforward than one might think. There is the distinct possibility that education is led by jobs rather than the other way around. People may not attend school for jobs they do not see.

Fourth, economic concepts and metaphors have permeated educational thinking (McCloskey, 1990). For example, the ideas of markets and productivity have been applied to totally new areas. Governments and educators are urged to create and respond to markets. Corporate structure is taken as a model for school governance. And this intellectual influence extends deep into the social sciences, so that even when one analyzes social problems from a political perspective, the analyst may be using concepts that have migrated there from economics (Boyd, Crowson, & van Geel, 1994; Wong, 1994). A visible sign of this penetration of government by business concepts is "reinventing government," Clinton's primary governmental reform.

Attendant to these influences are four types of errors, errors commonly made by policymakers and the public alike: misunderstanding the economic system; misunderstanding the educational system; misunderstanding the fit between the two; and misapplying economic concepts. All four errors are abundant in education—which is not to say that economic concepts cannot be productively applied. In fact, I will argue that educational institutions share key features with economic institutions and that many proposed educational reforms would be seen as foolish if similar reforms were attempted in business. The mistake is not one of applying economic concepts to education but of applying them badly, without understanding the effects they are likely to have.

One of the anomalies of educational reform is that educators and students are not treated like other people. That is, modern economics treats investments in education as rational responses to a calculus of expected costs and benefits (Becker, 1993). Yet teachers and students themselves are not accorded this same calculative rationality that is used to justify educational expenditures in the first place. Presumptions of altruism, incompetence, and obedience are no more valid about teachers than about others.

In this book I concentrate on educational policies at the national level in the United States, though policies in some other countries will be discussed as well. Although each country is unique in its policy dynamics, there are similarities. Trends I analyze here, such as economic rationalism, are pervasive in Britain, Australia, New Zealand, the Netherlands and most other advanced countries (Boston, Martin, Pallot, & Walsh, 1996; Kelsey, 1995; Pusey, 1991). Although education is conceived as supportive of economic development in most countries, each country stands at a somewhat different place.

I do not deal much with the actual processes and dynamics of how policy is formed, which differs significantly from country to country. Policy formation in American education is similar to that in other domestic areas, though with its own peculiarities (Kingdon, 1984; Wirt & Kirst, 1982). Social problems are connected to facilitative politics and policies through the services of policy entrepreneurs, who advocate their favorite policies from politically advantageous positions. Entrepreneurs present ideas that appeal to politicians even when these ideas won't work (Krugman, 1994b).

Such a policy-formation process contrasts with either a fully rational policy process, in which problems are defined and appropriate policies invented (Lasswell, 1971), or an incrementalist process, in which policy drifts in small steps over periods of time, with policymakers "muddling through" (Braybrooke & Lindblom, 1970). The overall pattern is neither fully rational nor irrational. Unfortunately, often problems are not solved. In fact, there is a mismatch. The policies adopted don't do the job.

# CHAPTER 2

# REAGAN'S EDUCATION POLICIES

The 1980s will be known as the Reagan decade. Although the events of the 1990s have begun to erode the marks of that era, it is instructive to consider what happened in domestic policy. Many of the educational policy issues at the national, state, and local levels of government were set largely by the economic policies at the national level, even though the states themselves have been at the forefront of the educational reform initiatives.

In prior decades other factors seemed more important in determining educational possibilities. The civil rights movement and its attendant policies of desegregation and affirmative action, the Great Society and its categorical funding programs, and the Vietnam War and its civil disorders all shaped education in the 1960s and 1970s. The big policies were social policies, political policies, war policies. But in the 1980s, national economic policies became the dominant force.

Until the beginning of the 1980s, the liberal economic view of education prevailed. This view holds that if one increases the educational attainment and achievement of students, even poor students from minority backgrounds, they will eventually secure better jobs, advance themselves socially, and help the economy. Education of the individual is a major driving force behind general economic improvement. This belief informed Lyndon Johnson's Great Society and is accepted readily by most educators. Research support for such faith in education is provided by studies showing positive relationships among educational attainment, achievement, and higher income (e.g., Berlin & Sum, 1988).

During the 1980s this argument for education was transformed. Conservatives contraposed the human capital argument by saying that the reason students could not get jobs was because of poor education. Terrel Bell, Reagan's first education secretary, said,

> I knew of the disquiet about the vanished American spirit, of industries in trouble. Why were so many people having so much difficulty finding jobs? It was because so many lacked the basic skills to be retrained. Where were we going to find the technically and scientifically informed people for an increasingly complex world of work?

> . . . Our loss of zest and drive and spirit would not be regained until we renewed and reformed our schools. (Bell, 1988, pp. 114–115)

Students came to be seen as not simply uneducated but as undisciplined—the fault of educators, the students themselves, their families, and lax government policies—and this new vision led to quite different educational policies. Mr. Peepers, polishing his glasses, was brushed aside by Joe Clark armed with a baseball bat.


## POLICY IN THE 1980s

Without question, the most influential social policy book of the 1980s was Charles Murray's *Losing Ground: American Social Policy 1950–1980* (1984). In a book laced with statistics, Murray put forth a bold thesis: The social programs of the Great Society had made the plight of the poor, especially poor blacks, *worse* than before. The book became a favorite in the Reagan White House. George Gilder, champion of free-enterprise economics, said, "For make no mistake, Murray has unleashed the most devastating sustained attack ever made against the welfare state" (Hume, 1985, p. 1).

Murray's (1984) argument was that indicators of well-being for the poor took a turn for the worse after the Great Society legislation in 1965 because the government's liberalized social policies made it profitable for the poor to behave in the short run in ways that were destructive to themselves and society in the long run. In spite of billions spent to eliminate poverty, the number of people in poverty declined, it then leveled off in the 1970s. In spite of massive efforts to provide job training, there remained a sizable hard-core unemployed group, mostly young black males. In spite of intense government efforts in education, achievement test scores worsened. Being unemployed and poorly educated, many young black males turned to crime. Crime rates rose dramatically. Furthermore, the number of illegitimate births and female-headed households soared, so that the poverty cycle was repeated.

The cause of this decline, according to Murray (1984), was that government programs had given the poor too much. His solution was to scrap the entire welfare and income-support structure for working-age persons, so that the only alternative was the job market. In Murray's words, "The tangible incentives that any society can realistically hold out to the poor youth of average abilities and average industriousness are mostly penalties, mostly disincentives. 'Do not study, and we will throw you out; commit crimes, and we will put you in jail; do not work, and we will make sure that your existence is so uncomfortable that any job will be preferable to it.' To promise much more is a fraud" (p. 177).

In Murray's (1984) scenario education still played a key societal role. It was indicted for failing to adequately educate poor people, who left school without job skills and took odd jobs, but not reliably or for long. Eventually these young people turned to drugs and crime as a way to make money and formed teenage gangs prowling the streets. They had children without proper financial support, abandoned them or became mothers on welfare. The young were not only uneducated but undisciplined.

Murray (1984) supported his argument by analyzing statistics (on poverty, employment, wages, education, crime, family) for poor blacks from before 1965 to 1980. After the favorable media blitz, scholars began criticizing Murray's analyses. In examining the educational data it was discovered that Murray had used the wrong statistic (the ratio of raw means) and that when the correct statistic (the standard deviation) was used, his argument that educational achievement for blacks had declined from 1965 to 1980 was wrong (House, 1985; House & Linn, 1986). In fact, black test scores improved relative to white test scores over this period, though by no means did they catch up (Burton & Jones, 1982). Murray's analysis of poverty was also strongly criticized (Danzinger & Gottschalk, 1985; Greenstein, 1985).

Some of Murray's (1984) most damaging evidence focused on unemployment among young black males. He was correct in stating that the employment problems of young black males had worsened since 1965, but wrong in asserting that older black males and white males had no employment problems. Labor force participation for all males had dropped since 1965. In fact, labor force participation for white and black males peaked in 1956 at 85.6% and 85.1%, respectively, went into a steady decline, and was 78.2% and 71.5% by 1980—a huge change (House & Madura, 1988).

The employment problems of young black and white males resulted from sweeping changes in the job market and, secondarily, the revolution in female employment. Blue-collar jobs and full-time jobs became a smaller portion of the job market, even while white-collar and part-time jobs increased tremendously. Women obtained a higher proportion of all jobs than before, and sometimes in occupational categories dominated by males. For example, between 1967 and 1982, white-collar jobs as a percentage of all jobs increased from 48.8% to 56.8%; blue-collar jobs decreased from 38.0% to 29.0%; and service jobs increased slightly from 13.2% to 14.2% of all jobs (House & Madura, 1988). These are large changes in the job market in a short period. The significance of these shifts is that it is mostly in the blue-collar jobs that males are employed, particularly black males in large cities. These jobs have been decreasing in proportion to other jobs.

These changes in the job market interacted with another phenomenon—the increasing numbers of women who were seeking employment. From 1965 to 1980 no fewer than 16.6 million additional women entered the labor market in the United States. The labor force participation rate of white women skyrocketed from 38.1% to 51.6%; that of black women increased from 48.6% to 53.4%. By

1986, the female labor participation rate was 55% (House & Madura, 1988). At the same time, there was a significant increase in the number and proportion of white-collar and service jobs, particularly clerical jobs, where females have traditionally sought employment. These were phenomenal changes in the composition of the work force.

The educational achievement of blacks actually improved substantially vis-à-vis that of whites (Burton & Jones, 1982). Although reading and math achievement stayed about the same for all students, minority scores improved. Blacks scoring at the "adept" reading level increased from 8% to 26% between 1975 and 1988 (Linn & Dunbar, 1990), and comparative gains were recorded for blacks in math and science, though not for Hispanics (Educational Testing Service [ETS], 1990a). Nor did the educational achievement data portend signs of a black educational underclass. The lower end of the black achievement distribution did not display evidence of a low-achieving group split off from the mainstream of black students. There may be an underclass, but it was not foreshadowed by a group of low-achieving students separated in educational achievement from the rest (Madura, 1990).

The scenario in which poor education led to unemployment and poverty and then to welfare and crime is demonstrably incorrect. This is not to say that education for poor blacks is good or that it is the equal of whites or that math and science education are as good as in other countries or that education should not be made better. It is to say that educational achievement for poor blacks has not declined precipitously (ETS, 1990b), and that if there is an underclass, it probably stems from causes other than poorer education, the most probable causes being the changing job structure, loss of manufacturing jobs, chronic unemployment, and withdrawal of males from the labor market. Education can and should be made better but its deterioration is not the root of our social problems.

## BIG POLICY

The real causes of unemployment and social distress can be traced to economic policies. Both the Johnson and Nixon administrations pursued expansionary and inflationary policies, one to support a war and the other to win reelection. Beginning with inflation generated by the Vietnam War, the United States entered a long period of relative economic decline (Gilpin, 1987). In the 1950s the United States accounted for 40% of gross world product; in 1986, for 13%. Real income peaked in 1973, and income distribution became more unequal (Levy, 1987a & b).

This national economic deterioration accelerated during the Reagan years. The Reagan administration pursued economic policies that reduced taxes and greatly increased expenditures on the military, thus incurring the largest national debt in history. The expansionist policy of incurring a huge deficit stimulated the economy in the early 1980s but also damaged the country's international trade. Furthermore, inequality of income and wealth among Americans increased dramatically.

Kevin Phillips (1990), Nixon's former political strategist, plotted the dimensions of this new inequality: "By several measurements, the United States in the late twentieth century led all other major industrial nations in the gap dividing the upper fifth of the population from the lower—in the disparity between top and bottom" (p. 8). In 1981, the top 1 percent of taxpayers had 8.1% of total reported income; by 1986, they had 14.7%. From 1977 to 1987, the top 1 percent of family after-tax income went from $174,498 to $303,900, a 74.2% increase. The bottom 10 percent went from $3,528 to $3,157, a 10.5% decrease. This trend continued. By 1989, the average income of the upper 1 percent was $559,000, and by 1993 $800,000, compared with $8,400 for the bottom fifth.

Between 1981 and 1988, the net worth of the 400 richest Americans tripled. The pay of chief executives of corporations rose from 35 times the average of worker income in the 1970s to 120 times in the 1990s, compared with 20 times in Japan and 35 times in Britain (Crystal, 1991). The ratio of the upper 10% of worker wages to the lowest 10% of wages was 5.6 to 1 in the United States, compared with 3.4 in Britain and France, 2.7 in Japan, 2.4 in Germany, and 2.2 in Sweden (*Economist*, 1994). During these years the richest 1 percent received 60% of *after-tax* income. Stanford economist Paul Krugman commented, "Where did all that extra income go? The answer is that it all went to the very top" (quoted in Nasar, 1992, p. A1). Furthermore, inequality of income is *negatively* related to increases in labor productivity and growth in GDP per capita (*Economist*, 1994e, pp. 20–21).

Although the poor have been hurt most, the middle classes have also been squeezed (DeMott, 1990; Ehrenreich, 1990; Phillips, 1993). The upper 20% of families had 51.4% of all pretax income by 1989, leaving the other half of the national income to be split among the other 80%. Medical costs soared. The financial squeeze on the middle classes led to taxpayer rebellions and eventually the election of Clinton in a populist reaction. Previously, Republicans associated Democrats with minorities, thus persuading large numbers of middle-class whites to vote for Reagan and Bush (Edsall & Edsall, 1991). In the 1994 congressional elections the Republicans captured large numbers of white voters and both houses of Congress.

In this increasing inequality, the United States is certainly not alone, though it may be first.

For 40 years after 1930 the gap between rich and poor in America narrowed. Since the end of the 1960s it has been widening, and is greater now than at any time since the creation of the modern welfare state. . . . a similar trend is apparent in many other industrial countries. . . . Why has inequality increased? A large part of the answer lies

with the liberal economic policies adopted in many parts of the world in the past 15
years. Many governments have cut tax rates for the rich and restrained spending on
benefits for the poor. . . . In recent years the economic forces of international competition and (above all) new technology have gathered strength. ("Slicing the cake," 1994,
p. 13)

Four Reagan policies accounted for much of the shift in income distribution:
tax rate reduction, federal budget management, deregulation, and monetary and
debt policy (Phillips, 1990). The top federal income tax bracket was slashed from
70% to 28% under Reagan. At the same time, the social security tax doubled,
from $1,500 to $3,000 on an income of $40,000, which increased the tax burden
of moderate incomes but was of little consequence to higher incomes. The effect
was that the rich paid much less, and the moderate and poor income earners paid
more. The percent of the federal budget spent on human resources declined from
28% to 22%, while defense spending rose from 23% to 28%, contributing to an
altered distribution pattern.

Deregulation led to wheeling and dealing and the making of vast sums of
money, the savings and loan debacle being the most visible episode. In 1987, Michael Milken, the junk bonds dealer, made $550 million. In addition, the federal
government pursued high interest rate policies, which favored creditors over debt-
ors, partly to entice foreign investors to buy bonds that financed the burgeoning
debt. In 1976, Japan bought $197 million in treasury bonds; in 1986, it bought
$138 billion. This influx of foreign funds allowed the Reagan administration to
expand the military and stimulate domestic consumption simultaneously, but at
long-term cost.

These policies exacerbated the county's international financial and trade position. The federal government borrowed huge sums at high interest rates to finance the debt. In 1980, the United States had a trade surplus of $166 billion.
On Reagan's last day in office, it had a debt to foreigners of $500 billion (Phillips,
1990). In 1987, Japan surpassed the United States in total national assets ($43.7
to $36.2 trillion), whereas a few years before it had been much less wealthy. In
terms of per capita gross national product, the United States was ninth in the
world. In the late 1980s the government was forced to devalue the dollar to bolster
foreign trade to cut the trade deficit, and everything became cheap to foreign nations.

Many economists thought the future disconcerting. The competitiveness of
many sectors of the economy had been damaged. In a vicious cycle a declining
economy forced the United States to borrow to finance its deficit, and the bor-
rowing forced industries into further decline, since the large interest payments ab-
sorbed capital that should have been used for reinvestment. By 1990, interest on
the national debt was second in size only to defense in the federal budget, and
debt interest would soon be the largest budget item.

While commentators debated the historical thesis that great powers decline because of imperial overreach on defense spending (Kennedy, 1987), political economists were blunt about the international consequences: "American mismanagement of its own internal affairs and of the international financial system caused the responsibilities of the hegemon to fall largely upon the Japanese" (Gilpin, 1987, p. 340). A new international economic order emerged with a humbler role for the United States.

Internally, the rich had become richer—especially the very wealthy—the poor had become poorer—the homeless on the streets being most visible—and the middle classes strained to maintain their standard of living. They did this by expanding personal credit and spouses going to work as did the working classes. But there was a limit to increasing family income this way. In general, the middle classes became more insecure (DeMott, 1990; Ehrenreich, 1990).

## LITTLE POLICY

Where did the effects of these economic policies leave education? In the accepted liberal scenario, improved education leads to improved job skills, employment, and a healthy economy, including international competitiveness. Liberals still wanted to increase educational spending. However, if something was wrong, and it seemed there was, it was a short step to the conservative scenario: The failure of the educational enterprise, especially education of the poor, was a major cause of the national failures, domestic and international.

In the conservative analysis, inadequate education led to poor job skills, which led to unemployability and unemployment, which led to low wages and poverty, which led to welfare, family dissolution, and crime, and to a declining national economy. The failure of education resulted in defective students who could not or did not want to work. Their failure was not the fault of the society or of the economic structure, but of themselves, their families, and the educational system. Murray supplied statistics to accompany themes articulated by neoconservatives Irving Kristol, Norman Podhoretz, and Allan Bloom, who traced educational problems to the breakdown of authority in the 1960s. Students and workers were not only uneducated, they were undisciplined.

Given this interpretation, how could education be rescued? First of all, little new money was available from the federal government (after inflation). In spite of rhetoric about the centrality of education to the national welfare, the federal reforms proposed entailed no significant new costs: commonsense remedies, for example *What Works,* (U.S. Department of Education, 1986), cultural literacy, accountability through testing, new graduation and teacher certification requirements, and vouchers or schools of choice. None of these reforms cost much more than current expenditures.

The federal education agenda during the Reagan years turned from equity, access, social welfare, the common school, regulations, and federal intervention to excellence and performance standards, ability and selectivity, productivity, parental choice and institutional competition, deregulation, and state and local initiatives (Clark & Astuto, 1990). The Reagan policy agenda consisted of institutional competition, individual competition, performance standards, harder content, parental choice, and character building.

Secretary of Education Bell (1988) set the theme for the decade in 1983 with *A Nation at Risk.*

> Our Nation is at risk. Our once unchallenged preeminence in commerce, industry, and technological innovation is being overtaken by competitors. . . . [Education] undergirds American prosperity, security and civility. . . the educational foundations of our society are being eroded by a rising tide of mediocrity that threatens our very future as a nation and a people. If an unfriendly foreign power had attempted to impose on America the mediocre educational performance that exists today, we might well have viewed it as an act of war. (pp. 123–124)

Education was at fault, and Reagan campaigned on its failures. However, although the report called for increased expenditures for reform, after the election Reagan lost interest. "Those long time friends . . . had been telling me that the President's commitment to the school reform effort was inspired by political opportunism and that it would come to an abrupt halt after the 1984 election. I refused to believe them. . . . But with a sour taste in my mouth, I had to acknowledge that my friends had been right after all" (Bell, 1988, p. 158–159).

Between fiscal years 1980 and 1989, federal funds for elementary and secondary education declined 17%, after adjusting for inflation (National Center for Educational Statistics [NCES], 1990). From 1981 the Department of Education budget declined from 0.6% to 0.4% of the gross national product and from 2.5% to 1.8% of the federal budget (Clark & Astuto, 1990). Federally funded educational research also declined. Between 1980 and 1988 educational research and development (R&D) funding decreased by 33%. Although funding for federal research and development increased 24% during the Reagan years, the increase was in defense R&D. In fiscal 1987 defense accounted for 64% of the total federal R&D budget and education for 0.2% (General Accounting Office [GAO], 1988).

By 1985, Reagan had found a compatible Secretary of Education, William Bennett, who agreed that money was not the answer for education. Bennett was a strong advocate of cultural literacy, the view that students lack basic cultural knowledge that would make them successful, as defined by Hirsch (1987) and Bloom (1987). In their view liberal indulgence had resulted in the destruction of the curriculum in the public schools and universities under pressure from minority groups. Cultural literacy demanded a return to the classic works that formed the intellectual core of Western civilization.

Furthermore, Bennett and Assistant Secretary Chester E. Finn, Jr., saw national testing as a means by which national goals could be achieved (Ravitch & Finn, 1987). Students and teachers could be held accountable by imposition of new tests and standards of excellence. Bennett used the "Wall Chart" to compare states on SAT scores, and comparisons of states on National Assessment of Educational Progress (NAEP) scores received high priority.

On the other hand, state funding for education did increase substantially during the 1980s. Across the states as a whole, real revenues per pupil rose 31% between 1980 and 1988, although this varied tremendously from state to state (Odden, 1989). These increases coincided with an expansionary economic period, and policy analysts attributed the increases to both the economic expansion and state reforms (Firestone, Fuhrman, & Kirst, 1989). By 1991, however, the United States was entering a recession, and most states faced large budget deficits and cutbacks in education (Tolchin, 1991).

The governors became more active in state educational politics, interested primarily in the link between education and their states' economic competitiveness. Big business became more involved, and the businessmen with the most influence were those representing multinational corporations. National organizations also increased their influence (Mazzoni, 1994). Organizations like the Educational Commission of the States, the National Conference of Legislatures, the Council of Chief State School Officers, the Carnegie Corporation, and especially the National Association of Governors served to nationalize a common set of reform ideas.

Although the focus was on devolution of responsibility for education to state and local units, and governors and legislators initiated most reforms, state policies in general mirrored the federal agenda and reinforced federal preferences through traditional state agency activities—monitoring, inspecting, and enforcing standards (Astuto & Clark, 1986). Of three kinds of accountability—public control by officials and politicians, professional control by teachers and educators, and consumer control through partnerships and market mechanisms (Kogan, 1986)—emphasis was placed on the first and last (Guthrie, 1990). Most reforms were designed to cost little new money (though some states provided more), discipline students and teachers, and protect upper- and middle-class interests.

Most states instituted achievement testing programs as centerpieces of reform. Testing was relatively inexpensive and, in the views of governors and legislators, promised to discipline students and teachers to increase achievement. It was an easy way to hold educators accountable for results. Forty-seven states started testing students; 39 tested teachers (ETS, 1990b). States also added requirements for high school graduation and teacher certification (Firestone et al., 1989). Little attention was paid to reduction of class size, teacher incentives, or redistribution of funding.

Cities also developed accountability plans. The most pervasive change in schools across the country was "establishing new consistently enforced codes of conduct," as well as stricter attendance policies, grade requirements, and more testing and homework, especially in schools with poor, minority students living in central city areas of high unemployment (ETS, 1990b, p. 10). For example, in 1981 New York City implemented the Promotional Gates Program, which required students who did not attain a certain reading test score to be retained at grade level until they did so. (The average elementary class size in New York City was 43 students; 80% of public school students in New York City were minorities.) During the first year 25,000 students were retained in fourth and seventh grades, and the city spent millions in remediation. However, subsequent evaluations indicated that test scores did not improve any more than with other special programs (Office of Educational Evaluation, 1982).

Vouchers and schools of choice were also advocated. Proponents believed that competition would force schools to become more accountable to clients, just as businesses were accountable to customers in the deregulated airline, telephone, and savings and loan industries. Advocates saw many benefits (Chubb, 1988; Chubb & Moe, 1990), despite strong criticisms (Glass & Matthews, 1991; Kirst, 1990). These ideas appealed to the middle classes, who saw their children trapped in school districts with decreasing resources and increasing numbers of minority students. How else could they guarantee their children a superior education, the basis of middle-class advancement, in such an insecure environment?

Through schools of choice the middle classes might be able to achieve insulation and advantage for their children, even as their own resources were stretched. Choice plans were considered in several states and cities. For example, in 1990 Oregon voted on a plan to provide $2,500 in tax credits for students enrolled in private schools or educated at home (defeated 2 to 1), and Felix Rohatyn (1990) recommended that New York City adopt a voucher plan with $3,000 of public money going to each student in a private school. Since it is difficult to imagine a poor mother shopping for a school at which she would have to absorb half the costs, these plans seemed aimed at the upper and middle classes.

By the end of the decade, governance restructuring schemes were popular, such as decentralization of the Chicago schools, brought about by a disgusted Illinois legislature. This plan called for control of each school by a local council composed of parent, teacher, and public members with power to fire the principal. The architect of the plan, Don Moore, called it the most far-reaching reform of big city schools in 20 years (Johnson, 1988). Most restructuring reforms were less radical, consisting of "site based management." Counterintuitively, the strong emphasis on accountability at the top sometimes opened possibilities at the ground level.

Educational research tended to be reactive rather than proactive, playing a subsidiary rather than a formative or challenging role. In other words, the content of much research was determined by the reforms rather than vice versa. Funded educational research followed government policy, with research on testing increasing. The National Center for Educational Statistics (NCES), which funded the National Asessment of Educational Progress, received more funding, and test development was the mission of the largest R&D center (Sroufe, 1991).

The reforms were initiated by combined efforts of media and government. Few reforms were researched in advance, and many were contrary to research evidence. Research funding seemed to follow the government reforms, and research followed the funding. Whatever one might say about policy affecting educational practice, government policy does have a strong influence on the direction of research.

## CONCLUSION

The economic policies of the Reagan administration, of simultaneously reducing taxes and greatly increasing military expenditures, thereby incurring a huge national debt, shifted large sums of money from the poor and middle classes to the wealthy and eroded the international economic position of the United States. The schools were blamed for much of the consequences, and the steadfast liberal belief that economic productivity depends on improving basic skills led educators to accept the blame. Conservatives pointed to undisciplined students, teachers, and workers as sources of the problems.

> In talking to these commission members, as I have done, one is struck by two facts. First, they think they know who the villains are: inadequate teachers, irresponsible parents, irrelevant or inadequate curricula, unmotivated students from whom too little is expected or demanded, an improvement-defeating bureaucracy, a lowering of standards for promotion and graduation, and a lack of competitiveness that would serve as a goad for schools to take steps to improve themselves. I use the word villain advisedly. (Sarason, 1990, pp. 13–14)

Many educational policies of the 1980s were attempts by federal, state, and local governments to deal with crises by disciplining students and teachers through tougher regulations and standards, by adding requirements and achievement testing, and by intensifying competition among students and organizations. Other reforms, such as decentralization and schools of choice, attempted to change the basis of school governance. The reforms had in common that they cost little, were meant to discipline students, and protected the interests of the middle and upper classes.

Would these policies work? There are two considerations. First, could such policies be successfully implemented? Those who have studied school reforms over the past decades said "Probably not." Most reforms do not take sufficient account of how schools operate (Elmore & McLaughlin, 1988). For the most part, the reforms focused on monitoring or coercion but were devoid of ways to improve internal operations. For example, a probable outcome of high-stakes testing is that the teachers will teach the tests, leading to higher test scores and lower educational achievement concurrently (Ellwein, Glass, & Smith, 1988).

Central authorities have not been successful in implementing reforms in the past because the reforms are detached from the substance of schooling. On the other hand, there assuredly would be outward acceptance of the new reforms, with teachers and administrators complying with rules. The result traditionally has been cosmetic changes, at which the schools excel.

Second, if these policies were implemented, would they be successful in reversing the perceived national decline? Would they reverse the nation's economic difficulties and make law-abiding, economically self-sufficient citizens out of the poor? One cannot be certain, but the most reasonable answer is "Not likely." Improving the work force requires more than pressuring teachers and students, and if the work force were "disciplined," what difference would it make? Is an undisciplined work force the primary problem? Increasing educational skills to ensure economic productivity and civil harmony is only part of the problem.

In the 1970s and 1980s, when economic productivity slowed, the American economy put a higher share of its resources into education than in the 1950s, but productivity declined anyhow (Krugman, 1992). Productivity decline resulted from bureaucratization, bad business management, lack of investment in R&D, and lethargy in adopting new production techniques. To put the issue another way, a male in the 84th percentilie in math achievement in 1986 earned 8% *less* than one at the 16th percentile in 1978 (Levin, 1993a). The increase in schooling between 1929 and 1982 accounted for about one-quarter of the increase in per capita income (Becker, 1993). Education is an important factor in productivity but not the dominant factor and certainly not the sole factor. In spite of faith in education, education cannot substitute for intelligent economic policies, or compensate for destructive ones.

Nonetheless, even though poor education did not lead to the economic and social woes of the country, there is a role for education to play in increasing equality and productivity. Both the preservation of democracy and successful economic development require better educated citizens. Although education did not cause the national decline, it might help forge a way out. However, educators and the public must adopt a more enlightened view of the role of education, of what it can and cannot do, in contrast to the naive faith that has characterized the past, a simple faith that makes education a scapegoat for every ill that besets the nation.

# CHAPTER 3

# CLINTON'S EDUCATION POLICIES

In the mid-1990s the Clinton administration faced difficult economic and social conditions. Ordinarily, liberal governments want to spend more money on education and social services, but no large sums of money were available because of the huge national debt. The budget agreement negotiated between President Bush and the Democratic Congress in 1990 limited discretionary spending to $540 million with no allowance for inflation, though mandatory social spending such as Social Security and Medicare could continue to rise. Clinton faced constraining financial conditions, although he had entered office with a mandate for change.

At the beginning of his administration Clinton was not afraid to challenge upper-class interests by moderately raising income tax rates on the wealthy, but also pledged no new taxes on the middle classes, a constituency that thought itself hard pressed. And he fought for the North American Free Trade Agreement and World Trade Organization legislation against labor and environmental interests. Even though Clinton was interested in social equality, he had to find ways to satisfy middle-class and business interests. And it was clear from his 1992 campaign that he had no desire to be identified too closely with black political interests and anti-poverty programs (Edsall & Edsall, 1991).

At the same time he quietly added $21 billion in tax credits for low-wage earners, a substantial sum, and funds for the homeless were doubled to $1.5 billion. These efforts were framed as helping middle-class workers rather than "fighting poverty" (DeParle, 1994). Administration officials said privately it would be "counterproductive" to talk too much about ghetto residents because such talk might provoke a backlash among whites.

Since the New Deal, liberals have traditionally assigned government a strong role in solving social problems, which encourages government centralization and expansion. New efforts to reorganize, coordinate, integrate, and regulate were pursued, though Clinton's "neoliberal" policies also called for privatization of some government functions. Four directions in education policy emerged: a reordering of priorities within budget constraints; promulgating national educational standards; linking education more closely to work; and "reinventing" government through encouraging market relationships between government and private organizations. This last strategy distinguished Clinton as a "new" Democrat or neoliberal.

Shifting money within the budget was possible initially since Democrats controlled Congress and the presidency the first two years. However, the 1995 Clinton budget was only slightly different from previous Republican budgets (Garcia & Gonzalez, 1995; Rosenbaum, 1994). Changes were made in 1 percent of the budget, less than $20 billion in a $1.5 trillion budget, including modest increases in education, job-training, public works, and scientific research.

During the first year the Department of Education attempted to reform student loans and focus money for the disadvantaged on poorer school districts, without significantly increasing the overall budget. In 1994 Congress passed two bills to "create a better-educated work force to face increasing global competition: one would stress educational achievement, and the other would link schools to businesses" (Manegold, 1994). The Goals 2000 legislation earmarked $422 million to establish voluntary national educational standards and set the year 2000 as the date on which American students should be first in the world in math and science. The "Schools-to-Work Transition" bill provided $300 million in 1995 and lesser amounts later to forge closer links between business and schools.

National standards legislation was a discernible shift toward centralization. Ernest Boyer, U.S. Commissioner of Education in the late 1970s, said, "If I had ever whispered national standards, I think I would have lost my job. . . . Within a decade we have gone from this preoccupation of local control to national standards" (Celis, 1994, p. B7). The rationale for the legislation came from the belief that other countries were doing a better job of training students for work, which made these countries more competitive economically. Clinton anticipated another $1.7 billion the following two years, but his plans were curtailed by the 1994 Congressional elections in which the Republicans took over Congress and engaged him in a budget impasse (Celis, 1994).

In previous decades the Education Department had acquired a reputation for incompetence. Reagan wanted to abolish the department altogether (established under Carter) but relegated it to basement status after lobbying by proponents (Bell, 1988). However, during the Reagan–Bush years the department lost 33% of its work force, 5,023 people were left by 1994 (Winerip, 1994b). A General Accounting Office review claimed the Department was "impaired," had a "negative self-image," "suffers from management neglect," and was "a dumping ground for staff and equipment that other agencies did not want" (Winerip, 1994b, p. A1). Demoralization did not improve performance.

For instance, the federal higher education loan program handled by the department was a debacle. For several years the government had been losing $4 billion a year in fraud and defaults, a significant portion of the department's $29 billion budget. Proprietary schools accounted for 76% of the loan defaults, and the department had no effective way of rectifying these losses. A student could apply for 10 different Pell grants simultaneously without the department knowing.

However, it was primarily the private and for-profit schools that ripped off the government, not students, who often did not see any of the money loaned on their behalf. The money went directly to the schools. When the department tried to crack down on fraudulent schools, congressmen and senators leaped to the defense of schools in their jurisdictions and religious schools with which they identified, some of the worst offenders (Winerip, 1994a).

Reforming the Education Department itself presented a formidable challenge. It was difficult to see how bold new national educational initiatives could emerge from the department since it could muster neither the money nor the agency capabilities to provide leadership. Nonetheless, in spite of these impairments, the Clinton administration announced grand plans for national education reform.

## NATIONAL GOALS, STANDARDS, AND TESTING

One primary reform strategy relied on a standards-and-testing initiative. Both politics and particular leaders made such an approach likely. Clinton installed a testing reform when he was governor of Arkansas, and his first Secretary of Education, Richard Riley, instituted a similar program as governor of South Carolina (Cibulka, 1991; Riley, 1995; Stevenson, 1995). Raising educational standards through testing appealed to the middle classes, partly for what it meant in gaining access to better jobs for their children, and also because for some it was a code word for restricting minority access. Although the standards-and-testing strategy of school reform was initiated under Bush, it became a centerpiece of the Clinton administration.

In "World Class Standards for American Education," the argument for national standards and assessment was made succinctly:

> Standards are a definition of what students should know and be able to do. Establishing clear standards both raises expectations and lets everyone in the education system know what to aim for. Teachers, students, and parents should know what is expected for success. . . .
>
> The purpose of having standards is to raise the achievement of all students and to ensure that all students have equal educational opportunity. Almost every other modern society has established standards for what students should learn. Having good standards means setting higher expectations for students. Students will learn more when more is expected of them, in school and at home. . . .
>
> In the absence of national standards, a haphazard, accidental national curriculum has evolved based on standardized multiple-choice tests and mass market textbooks. . . . When no one agrees on what students should learn, then each part of the

educational system pursues different, and sometimes contradictory, goals. As a result, the education system as a whole is riddled with inequity, incoherence, and inefficiency.

If we have good national standards, many parts of the educational system will change to reflect those standards:

- Textbooks will change to emphasize student understanding;
- Student assessments will change to test whether students understand what they have learned;
- Instructional methods will change to emphasize reasoning and problem-solving;
- Teacher education will change and professional development will change so that all teachers are prepared to teach to higher standards; and
- New technologies will be used to increase learning to meet the new standards. (U.S. Department of Education, 1992)

Presumably, the new standards would be based on pursuit of the six national education goals, later expanded to eight (U.S. Department of Education [USDE], 1991, 1992):

- All American children will start school ready to learn;
- At least 90 percent of our students will graduate from high school;
- Our students will demonstrate competency in challenging subject matter and will learn to use their minds well, so they may be prepared for responsible citizenship, further learning, and productive employment;
- American students will be first in the world in science and mathematics achievement;
- Every adult will be literate and have the knowledge and skills necessary to compete in a world economy and exercise the rights and responsibilities of citizenship;
- Every school will be safe and drug-free and offer a disciplined environment conducive to learning (USDE, 1992);
- The Nation's teaching force will have access to programs for the continued improvement of their professional skills and the opportunity to acquire the knowledge and skills needed to instruct and prepare all American students for the next century;
- Every school will promote partnerships that will increase parental involvement and participation. (*National Education Goals Panel*, 1994)

These national goals focused on productivity and discipline. (For the direct connection between the Clinton programs and human capital as seen by the administration, see Smith & Scoll, 1995.) There is no mention of equality or equity. If the argument for standards is correct—that what is specified directly and assessed quantitatively will improve—one would not anticipate increased equality or equity. Rather, global economic competition has center place.

In the standards reform, there are three types of standards: performance standards, indicating how well students and schools should do; content standards, indicating what subject matter should be taught and learned; and opportunity-to-learn standards, which outline the conditions schools or other educational organizations must meet to ensure that students have an opportunity to achieve the performance standards (Elmore & Fuhrman, 1995). These last standards attempt to address the inequality issue. Opponents argued that adding another set of rules and regulations called opportunity standards is no more likely to help than have those of the past.

The Clinton administration started to establish an appartus to implement these standards, mostly through quasi-governmental organizations and tying funding, such as funding for disadvantaged students, to such standards. Goals 2000 legislation provided for the National Education Goals Panel and the National Education Standards and Improvement Council, the purpose of which was to promote goals and high standards throughout the country. However, the Republican-dominated Congress thought this too much federal intrusion in public education, always considered a state responsibility. The standards council did not pass, and the standards had to be made voluntary (Smith, 1995).

One especially influential version of the standards-and-testing strategy was advanced by the New Standards Project of Lauren Resnick and Marc Tucker (1992). In their view the key to change was a European-style examination system that would "measure student progress toward meeting world class standards . . . in such a way that employers . . . would be likely to use it as the basis of employment decisions" (p. 6). Such an exam system would provide a powerful incentive for students to study hard. The exams would define the work that students would be asked to do, and all students would be expected to meet the same standards, which would be "benchmarked" to the highest in the world. "One either meets the standard set by the exams or does not: there are no grades or scores making a smooth curve from 'fail' to 'excellent,' though 'pass' and 'pass with distinction' would be allowed" (*New Standards*, 1992, p. 7).

The national standards would be developed by identifying "competitor nations," analyzing the curricula in those countries, describing the performance of foreign students, estimating the percentage of students who met the performance standards (benchmarking), and incorporating these performances into American exams. Several exams would be developed by consortia of states and equated to one another. Exam development would occur in several subject matters and grade levels. Then teams of teachers would be trained in the new standards and exams, and these teams would train other teams, so that the new standards would "cascade" throughout the educational system. Eventually, classrooms, teachers, and materials would conform to the new standards.

At least one state governor was deeply impressed with the Goals 2000 approach. Roy Romer announced that Colorado would not only join the national goals project but also reduce its waste diversion by 50% by the year 2000. He asked citizens to throw away one pound less of trash per day and enjoined state and local agencies to measure statewide progress toward that goal (Cuthbertson, 1994).

Arguments against using standards and testing as the engine of reform have been advanced by Koretz, Madaus, Haertal, and Beaton (1992), among many others, who argued that similar attempts have failed repeatedly in the past, that instruction would be narrowed and test scores artificially inflated to the point of questionable validity (by teaching to the tests), and that the new "performance" tests offered no way around these problems. Also, assessment costs would be much higher than anticipated (maybe $6 billion per year). Most who advocated standards and testing were not testing experts. However, many test experts fell into line when politicians endorsed the idea.

There are several difficulties with this approach. First, there are problems with whether consensus can be obtained on national goals and standards. The national goals were not produced through collaboration with educators or the public. (One source who should know told me Clinton himself wrote the national goals in a hotel room in Washington when he was governor of Arkansas and chair of the governors' association.)

> Teachers and administrators had little or no participation in the development of the President and governors' goals. . . . For goals to be effective, they must possess at least two characteristics. First, they must be agreed to and held as important; and second, they must be seen as within reach if great effort is made. At the moment, current goals appear to lack sufficient amounts of either characteristic. (Porter, 1990, pp. 39–40)

The content standards developed by the National Council of Teachers of Mathematics were well received. The science standards were less well received. The more the standards crept into social areas, the more controversy arose about their content. The national history standards were condemned 99 to 1 by the U.S. Senate, and local groups all over the country questioned the imposition of national standards. (The one dissenting senator wanted to take punitive action against the authors.)

A historian, writing in a conservative political journal, said of the history standards: "The Standards came into existence because of the widespread realization that young people are largely ignorant of history. Now that the project has borne fruit, it is clear that people have different ideas as to what students are ignorant of. . . . In light of this melee, the notion that nationally-mandated Standards are wise is mad" (McDougall, 1995, p. 43).

Technical questions about establishing testing standards were raised by the General Accounting Office (GAO). "GAO found that NAGB's [National Assessment Governing Board] standard-setting approach was procedurally flawed and

that interpretations . . . were of doubtful validity. . . . NAGB's governance structure and procedures neither ensure that technical issues will be recognized nor
require that technical considerations be addressed early in the policy formation
process. GAO thus concluded that there is substantial continuing risk that NAGB
may give NAEP technically unsound policy" (GAO, 1993, pp. 3, 5). NAGB was
established by Congress as a quasi-governmental agency to attend to such matters.

Actually, the problem was more fundamental, according to two leading test
experts. "In fact, there is little agreement on what performance standards are, how
they are best set . . . and what their relationship is or should be to details used in
scoring student performances" (Baker & Linn, 1993/94, p. 1). Agreement within
the testing community on the feasibility of such procedures was lacking. Nonetheless, in spite of such criticisms, the initiatives went ahead.

By 1994 the first findings on national goals became available, measured by
indicators selected to discern progress (though not tied to content standards still
under development):

> On the whole, our progress toward the National Education Goals has been modest,
> at best. Even in areas where we have made significant progress from where we started,
> such as mathematics achievement at Grades 4 and 8, our current rate of progress will
> not be sufficient to reach the ambitious levels specified in the National Education
> Goals. (*National Education Goals Panel*, 1994, pp. 21–22)

Given the looming failure of the national goals approach to achieve the Year
2000 goals, what did the National Education Goals Panel recommend that the
federal government do? More of the same.

The goals panel believes that

> 1. clear, measurable academic standards of student performance should serve as the
> centerpiece of education reform; and
> 2. if we are to meet the Goals by the end of the decade, an immediate priority is to
> improve the capacity of all levels of governance to collect and analyze essential data
> that will drive education improvement. (National Education Goals Panel, 1994, p. 60)

The admonition to collect more data in the belief that the data would "drive
education improvement" is a common but questionable idea. Who would take
seriously a plan to save the starving masses of Africa by collecting data? Or by
establishing nutritional standards as to what African children need (Howe, 1997)?
Surely something more would be required. Such thinking seems far removed from
how schools function. For example, economic indicators are useful to those engaged in business activities but they do not "drive" economic activity. Imagine
that the governor of a state decided to improve business by setting standards and
announced that "henceforth, all businesses in the state will achieve 20% profits."

One suspects that even other governors would find this idea a bit strange, though one cannot be sure.

Furthermore, the history of similar attempts in the past is not a happy one. The failures and difficulties encountered with reform through standards and testing have been have been documented repeatedly since such schemes appeared in Michigan, Florida, and other states in the 1970s and in cities like New York in the 1980s (Glass & Ellwein, 1986; House, Linn, & Raths, 1982; House, Rivers, & Stufflebeam, 1974; Tyler, Lapan, Moore, Rivers, & Skibo, 1978).

One prominent example is New York City in the early 1980s, mentioned earlier. Frank Macchiarola, then chancellor of the New York City schools, implemented a policy that no student could pass beyond the fourth or seventh grades without achieving a specific score on the citywide test. The standard was that the student would have to be held back (retained, flunked) at that grade level until the student obtained a score on the reading test within one year of the norm for fourth grade. A standard was also enforced for the seventh grade, with students required to obtain scores within one and a half years of the norm. This initiative was called the "Promotional Gates Program"; plans were to add other subject areas eventually so there would be many such tests.

The reasoning behind the new standard was that teachers and students were not trying hard enough. They were not sufficiently motivated to achieve in school. If one put pressure on both through threat of failure, teachers and students would try harder and achieve more. This strategy assumed lack of motivation on the part of teachers, students, and administrators. The 350,000-member parent association was opposed. Although the participating teachers were given training and materials to teach the failed students, who were put into small, special classes, it was assumed that teacher knowledge was available either from what teachers already knew or could learn in a short time.

This proved to be untrue. Many students could not attain these standards, even after an extra year of instruction in special classes (House, Linn, & Raths, 1982). It was estimated that a fair percentage would never attain the prescribed standard. The Promotional Gates Program began to look like the "Hoover Dam" program with hundreds of thousand of students held back at the fourth and seventh grade levels at enormous added cost to the school district. (The mayor's office was particularly upset because it supplied half the funding for the schools in New York City's novel funding arrangements.) Test scores did not improve beyond what they had for remedial programs already in place. The program was quietly abandoned with a minimum of publicity. (In fact, the quiet retreat was overshadowed by scandals in the chancellor's office.)

Another example is the measurement-driven reform in Arizona in which one-quarter of the teachers and one-half the administrators estimated that the benefits of the new testing were worth the time, effort, and money required to administer the program, about the same estimate as the benefits of the previous state testing program (Smith, Noble, Haag, Seck, & Taylor, 1994). However, in this case Arizona provided no resources for teacher training and professional development, a significant difference. (The "performance tests" used in Arizona also had serious measurement problems.)

In spite of many examples and studies that demonstrate formidable implementation problems and ineffective results, these accountability-through-testing schemes have proliferated. They fill a strong political need by promising reform of education for minor costs, even a reduction in costs. And they have been repeatedly embraced by both political parties. Politics seems to drive these reforms, and when objections are raised by testing experts that critical technical tasks cannot be accomplished, the experts are overridden.

Something similar occurred in Britain during the implementation of national assessment in the Thatcher and Major regimes. The Education Reform Act of 1988 called for national curricula and national assessment. National curricula were developed by the government, and the national assessment, begun in 1991, attempted to use performance assessments, similar to those recommended for the United States (Gipps, 1993). Many problems were encountered but one lesson was that the same assessment could not serve all purposes—formative, summative, and diagnostic—as has been proposed in the United States. Numerous problems led the British government to return to regular standardized tests.

When "alternative performance assessments" were employed, assessments closer to what students experience in classrooms than what standardized achievement tests assess, the costs in money and time were high. In Britain it took two weeks to administer some of the exams, and similar problems plagued American projects. For example, one of the few empirical studies of the costs of developing and administering science performance assessments in California estimated the costs to be 20 times that of standardized multiple-choice tests (Stecher & Klein, 1997).

Another difficulty with accountability-and-control schemes is that they often generate the opposite of what they intend. As McNeil (1986) found in her study of social studies classrooms,

> when the school's organization becomes centered on managing and controlling, teachers and students take school less seriously. They fall into a ritual of teaching and learning that tends toward minimal standards and minimal effort. This sets off a vicious cycle. As students disengage from enthusiastic involvement in the learning process, administrators often see the disengagement as a control problem. They then increase their attention to managing students and teachers. (p. xviii)

One can generalize this to rules and regulations broadly conceived. The more formalization, the more informal subversion (Hoggett, 1991).

Another example is the Camden, New Jersey, school district, the fifth poorest in the country. In the 1980s Governor Thomas Kean established a test-driven curriculum designed around a battery of tests. According to the principal of Camden High,

> we are entrapped by teaching to the tests. . . the state requires test results. It "mandates" higher scores. But it provides us with no resources in the areas that count to make this possible. So it is a rather hollow mandate after all, as if you could create these things by shouting into the wind. . . .
>
> What is the result? We are preparing a generation of robots. Kids who are learning exclusively through rote. We have children who are given no conceptual framework. They do not learn to think, because their teachers are straitjacketed by tests that measure only isolated skills. . . .
>
> In order to get these kids to pass the tests, they've got to be divided up according to their previous test results. . . . They take preliminary tests before they leave eighth grade. Eighty percent are failed, because of what has not been done for them in elementary school. So they enter high school labeled "failures." Their entire ninth grade year becomes test preparation. . . . They take the state proficiency exams in April of the ninth grade year. If they fail, they do it again in tenth grade. If they fail again, it's all remediation in eleventh grade. Already in the ninth grade kids are saying, "If I have to do this all again, I'm leaving." The highest dropout rate is in the first two years. (quoted in Kozol, 1991, pp. 143–144)

The result was counterproductive, including a dropout rate of more than 50%. Test scores rose for those who continued because the only things students studied were the tests. But the result was not education, in the view of the teachers. Although advocates contend that better tests will change this scenario, such claims are merely aspirations. Of the many things that poor children in Camden and East St. Louis could use to improve their education, more testing is not one of them.

In the opinion of standards-and-testing advocates, education is inadequate because teachers and students are unmotivated or confused about what they are supposed to teach and learn. Motivation and direction can be supplied by external standards enforced by tests and exams, which will pressure teachers and students to work harder. The exams will also communicate what students should know. As David Cohen (1995) says, standards may illuminate reform, but they cannot drive it. Only an extensive and expensive system of teacher training would provide the conditions for success.

My own judgment is that the problems of the educational system lie elsewhere, and that new goals, standards, and examinations are unlikely to lead to serious reform. Reform advocates misunderstand how schools, teachers, and students will respond. There is no reason to believe that such attempts will end in other than failure, as in the past, except that the scale of the enterprise may make the crash more resounding this time.

## SYSTEMIC REFORM

A somewhat different version of goal, standards, and testing reform is "systemic" change, as formulated by Marshall Smith, Deputy-Secretary of Education in the Clinton administration. Smith and O'Day (1991) attribute many school ills to lack of coordinated policy:

> A fundamental barrier to developing and sustaining successful schools in the USA is the fragmented, complex, multi-layered educational policy system in which they are embedded. . . . The policy generation machines at each level and within each level have independent timelines, political interests, multiple and changing special interest groups, and few incentives to spend the time and energy to coordinate their efforts. (p. 237)

In Smith and O'Day's opinion, these fragmented structures and uncoordinated efforts create mediocrity in resources and conservatism in instructional practices. Schools need a common vision as to what students should know and be able to do when they leave school, and this common vision, expressed in a general curriculum framework, should be supplied by each state. "The state would design and orchestrate the implementation of a coherent instructional guidance system. The cornerstone of such a system would be a set of challenging and progressive curriculum frameworks" (p. 261). Districts, schools, and teachers would work within this framework.

In a way, Smith and O'Day's (1991) analysis is a restatement of the problem: Policy is fragmented because of the many diverse interests that schools must serve, including national, state, local, professional, and public interests. Having a coherent vision is difficult because various interests do not want the same things from schools, and achieving a common vision and set of consensus goals is a formidable task because it requires reconciling conflicting interests. In other words, fragmentation exists because people have different ideas about what schools should do.

"The fragmentation of education policy and reform in this nation is the natural result of our political system's divided governance structures, single issue candidates and interest group politics. . . . These factors result in policy driven by compromise and bargaining rather than any uniform vision of change" (Fuhrman & Massell, 1992, p. 11). Again, to lament the disunity is to lament the existence of conflicting interests and purposes within the society as a whole. Interest-group politics exist because different interests are allowed to organize and express themselves within the political system.

How can a coherent vision be achieved? Fuhrman and Massell (1992) have recommended restructuring state governing mechanisms, for example, merging K–12 and postsecondary committees; and establishing new boards and positions for interagency collaboration, for example, accountability and oversight committees, which would set standards for educational practice. Achieving a common vision requires changes in the governing system itself. However, one must wonder if the governing reforms required as a precondition for educational reform are easier to achieve than the educational reforms themselves. Reforming state government seems as formidable a task as reforming schools. Nor would reforming state governments eliminate contesting interests.

In fact, more extreme examples of fragmentation can hardly be found than in the federal government itself. There is little coordination of educational policy across federal departments and agencies. For example, in a critical area like science, math, engineering, and technology education, more than 11 federal departments and agencies have 276 separate educational programs, and these programs are the outgrowth of each department's own aspirations and particular congressional backing.

In 1993 the Department of Education spent $340.9 million on math, science, engineering, and technology education, the National Science Foundation (NSF) spent $537.9 million, the Defense Department spent $526.7 million, Health and Human Services $464.1 million, and the Department of Energy $102.1 million (Expert Panel for Review of Federal Education Programs, 1993). These departments do not have a common vision of science, math, engineering, and technology education, to say the least. There is little or no coordination or oversight across agencies. The Federal Coordinating Council on Science, Mathematics, and Engineering Education (FCCSET) was established by President Bush to secure coordination among government agencies, and, not surprisingly, the first evaluation of these programs concluded that there was little cooperation (Expert Panel, 1993).

Certainly, attempts to coordinate education policies and programs should be encouraged because uncoordinated efforts are mind-boggling in their wastefulness and lend credence to the claim that big government cannot generate anything except waste. However, systemic policy would require enormous political effort to coordinate contending interests among agencies and departments within the executive branch and Congress. It is by no means certain that such efforts can be successful. The attitude of many bureaucrats is that after all is said and done, everything will remain the same—similar to the view held by teachers about school reform. At present the federal government lacks the ability to coordinate its own efforts.

Systemic reform also casts the states as prime movers, but one must wonder whether state governments are capable of such efforts. One high-profile endeavor, the National Science Foundation's Statewide Systemic Initiative (SSI), requires states to submit plans for improving science, math, engineering, and technology education, which are then subject to NSF approval. An early review reveals that the SSI program has produced mixed results (Shields, Corcoran, & Zucker, 1994). Are states capable of generating a coherent vision of education, even in clearly defined and high-priority areas? The federal government might have to take the initiative for coordinating systemic reform—if it can find direction for itself.

Another possibility is that these efforts will amount to symbolic reshuffling and have little effect on educational practices, somewhat like rearranging an organization chart. Cohen (1991) has illustrated that it is one thing to have good state policies and quite another to affect classroom practices. After observing a teacher teach the required California math curriculum, Cohen commented, "This new policy aspires to enormous changes in teaching and learning. It offers a bold and ambitious vision of mathematics instruction, a vision that took imagination to devise and courage to pursue. Yet this admirable policy does little to augment teachers' capacities to realize the new vision" (p. 121). Most reform strategies rely heavily on as yet unrealized "authentic assessments" to shape classroom practices, but there are reasons to think such assessments will not achieve the results anticipated.

Leading experts on implementation of reforms seem to harbor similar doubts about the efficacy of systemic change.

> But the entire fragmented apparatus of American government structure weighs against such ventures. . . . Bypassing government appeals to many partly because the prospects for streamlining seem so bleak. . . . Neither new exams nor new curricula would work unless teachers understood them, and as things now stand, most teachers would not. (Cohen & Spillane, 1993, pp. 77,79)

> It is difficult to sustain the notion that local districts are agents of a larger corporate structure, with its own goals and interests, when districts regularly receive strong signals from their own constituents about what the purposes of the system are. (Elmore, 1993, p. 109)

> Policy coherence as intended by reformers and policy makers ultimately is achieved or denied in the subjective responses of teachers—in teachers' social constructions of students. (McLaughlin & Talbert, 1993, p. 248)

Standards and testing strategies are attempts to centralize the educational system to some degree, protests notwithstanding. Clune (1993b) summarized arguments for and against a centralized national curriculum and concluded that such a curriculum is neither necessary nor sufficient for educational change and reform: "The statist-centralized version of systemic policy built around authoritative curriculum frameworks is fatally flawed on the two grounds: A common curriculum is difficult, if not impossible, to apply considering the immense diversity of American schooling, and a tolerable link between policy at the top and change at the bottom is all but unattainable" (p. 250).

## CONCLUSION

At the beginning of his administration, Clinton was limited in what he could do, at first by the constrained budget and economic conditions that he faced, then by the new Republican Congress, which wanted to reduce government severely. Room for maneuver came in what he had done in the past as governor of Arkansas: develop national standards and enforce them by national tests. Another initiative was for the federal government to lead the states in systemic reforms, with the states developing curriculum frameworks, standards, and tests through which state educational policies would be coordinated. Neither of these ideas cost much new money. However, consensus on standards has been hard to attain, and the development of new exams is much more difficult and expensive than many advocates realized. Again, economic constraints and issues seemed to define the policies of the Clinton administration, as they had with Reagan and Bush.

Of course, the idea of defining goals and objectives and aligning curriculum and learning experiences with assessments harks back to Ralph Tyler's objectives-based model, introduced in the 1950s (Tyler, 1989). Systemic reform is the objectives model of curriculum development and evaluation writ large for an entire state or society. However, Tyler expected professionals to construct the educational experiences, with technical assistance from measurement experts. Local professionals would arrive at a consensus among themselves within a school. Even the National Assessment of Educational Progress was a method for reporting to the public, not for pressuring teachers, in founder Tyler's view. "A national achievement test is no more the answer to improving educational quality than is a national curriculum" (Tyler, 1979, quoted in Porter, 1990, p. 21).

By contrast, systemic reform expects central government to provide the vision, or at least goals and standards, and to evaluate professionals on that basis. Establishing tight systemic connections among all these elements seems unlikely because of many difficulties, not the least of which are conflicting goals and interests. It might be possible for the government to monitor and evaluate in ways that might direct or redirect activities at the federal or state levels but that do not control local activities, except through establishing conditions for good practice. Stimulating, then evaluating, rather than pressuring through assessment, seems more feasible in a "loosely coupled" system. "The new federalism implies a close coupling of education and economy, whereas most empirical literature suggests a loose coupling" (Cookson, 1995, p. 407). Close-coupling is likely to remain an elusive fantasy of those who have been deprived of educational reform for too long.

# CHAPTER 4

# EDUCATION AND THE ECONOMY

In the Introduction, I suggested that national education policies are closely tied to economic considerations in at least four ways. First, economic policies and conditions directly affect education policies. Second, education policies are formulated to improve productivity and decrease school costs. Third, education is tied to the economy in general ways, for example, education leads to better jobs and more economic growth. And, fourth, economic concepts and metaphors penetrate educational thinking.

In previous chapters, in discussing Reagan and Clinton education policies, I have illustrated the connection between economic conditions and educational policy at the national level. In this chapter I discuss the third relationship: how education and the economy interact at the macro-level. In Chapter 5 (on reinventing government), I will show how popularized ideas from economics and business penetrate government thinking.

In this chapter, I first present the fundamental problem of economic productivity decline in the American economy, discuss briefly the reasons for it and the prospects, and, most importantly, what role education plays in the economy. I want to contend that the role of education is more complex than commonly believed. It is not simply the case that improved education leads to better jobs and a better economy. Rather, it is often the case that the jobs precede education in important ways.

## THE PRODUCTIVITY PROBLEM

Economic productivity is extremely important because "production has eliminated the more acute tensions associated with inequality. Increasing aggregate output is an alternative to redistribution," Galbraith wrote in *The Affluent Society* in 1958. Such ideas guided the Truman and Eisenhower administrations, as well as those of Kennedy, who said, "In short, our primary challenge is not how to divide the economic pie, but how to enlarge it" (Rowen, 1968, p. 114), and Johnson: "So long as the economic pie continues to grow, there will be few disputes about its distributions among labor, business, and other groups" (Kearns, 1976, p. 145). This has become standard American economic policy.

During the 1950s and 1960s American output per worker rose at an average annual rate of 2.8%, but after 1970 it rose at only 1.2% (Krugman, 1992). There are several explanations of why this productivity decline occurred, only one of which involves education directly. Most generally, the decline of productivity is attributed to the playing out of technologies developed during and after World War II, with new technologies not yet contributing to substantial growth; second, to sociological and cultural changes, such as erosion of the work ethic, changes in the role of women and family structure, the weakening of education, and the development of an underclass; third, to political impediments, such as excessive taxes and regulation (Krugman, 1992).

Other countries became more competitive, partly because of their research and development (R&D) investments. R&D expenditures and investment rates are major determinants of productivity (Krugman, 1992). The United States invests in plant and equipment one-half per worker what Germany does and one-third what Japan does (Thurow, 1992). Research and development spending as a percentage of the gross national product (GNP) is the same as in Germany and Japan, but when military R&D is subtracted, the United States falls to tenth place among nations.

Economists contrast the individualistic style of American management with the communitarian style of the Germans and Japanese (Thurow, 1992). American managers are more focused on maximizing short-term profits and do not take long-term perspectives on their businesses or employees, who are treated as costs to be minimized. Employees, for their part, tend to maximize their own salaries and consumption and feel little loyalty to their employers. By contrast, managers in Japan focus on long-term market share and treat employees as important stakeholders, invest in worker welfare, and receive cooperation in return. Worker turnover in the United States is 4% per month versus 3.5% per year in Japan (Thurow, 1992).

Also, American management is often blindly led by numbers. For example, the American consumer electronics industry was eliminated because Japanese firms established profit levels below what they knew American managers would accept. If a product's profit margin fell below 15%, Americans would drop that product line. By moving from one product to another the Japanese eliminated the entire American industry, then raised prices (Thurow, 1992). The short-term perspective of American business is fueled by quarterly reports to which executive careers and compensation are tied.

The decline in productivity is also attributed to administrative inefficiencies. There has been an enormous increase in the number of white-collar workers who process more data, though decisions might be better made on the shop floor. Instead of decreasing costs, in many places computerization has increased costs.

There is more information to assemble in more reports and more time spent preparing and reading reports—in short, more bureaucracy at the middle level. The larger the business enterprise the more it resembles government bureaucracies with many administrative layers. Every action must be approved at higher levels. (To complete a real estate loan transaction in Colorado requires 33 signatures, all of which are statements to government or business agencies.) "Down-sizing" and "reengineering" have eliminated many middle-level jobs in attempts to reverse this tendency.

American businesses have also been slow to adjust to the revolutionary production system pioneered by Toyota (Cohen, 1993; Womack, Jones, & Roos, 1990). Japanese plants in Japan require 16.8 hours to assemble a vehicle compared with 21.2 hours for Japanese plants in North America, 25.1 hours for American plants, and 36.2 hours for European plants. And this work is accomplished with fewer defects and in less space. The Japanese work in teams, make many more suggestions per worker, suffer less hierarchy, receive more training, and have less absenteeism. Japanese cars are fundamentally cheaper to make, and this difference cannot be overcome by cheaper capital and labor (Cohen, 1993).

This manufacturing superiority stems from the high-volume flexible system of production in which die presses can be changed in a few minutes so that short specialized runs of cars can be made, rather than dedicating permanent die presses to huge runs that cannot be changed easily, the basis of the Ford manufacturing system that revolutionized mass production in its own time. This innovation also means that line workers, rather than specialized management personnel, have responsibility for changing the tool dies on the line (Womack et al., 1990).

Assembly workers work in teams with more responsibility. Workers can stop the assembly line if they see a problem, their suggestions are valued, their welfare protected, and their knowledge considered an asset—a distinct change from the Ford system. The resulting quality of production is so high that corrections for defects are near zero, compared with 25% in American and European plants. The bureaucratic hierarchy is reduced and more power is distributed to the shop floor, which in turn requires different organization, treatment of workers, and supplier relationships.

This revolutionary production system requires radical changes in authority relationships not fully accepted by Americans or Europeans. However, some manufacturers, such as Ford, are adopting these methods, once Japanese auto manufacturers demonstrated that they could achieve the same results with American workers.

In the view of some, the government response to these economic challenges was confused and counterproductive: deregulation and distribution of income to the top; lowering social expenditures to cut government costs; attacking unions and professional groups to lower wages (Cohen, 1993). When in trouble, American businesses traditionally have resorted to cheap labor through immigration and moving jobs elsewhere. Even before the North American Free Trade Agreement, Ford had a plant in Hermosillo, Mexico, where workers made $2.35 per hour as opposed to $18 an hour in Detroit. American wages have not increased on average for the past 25 years, but this has not saved many businesses.

> With great resourcefulness, RCA sought cheap labor and high-end niches as its primary response to early Japanese competition at the lower end of consumer electronics. It got what it sought: good, cheap labor. It reinvested offshore, holding to its traditional approach to production and lost everything to the Japanese, who were not allowed to go abroad for cheapest labor and who instead managed to situate themselves on a new production trajectory. (Cohen, 1993, p. 146)

Instead of seeking cheap labor, the Japanese invested in innovative production techniques and new products.

## PROSPECTS

Opinions about the economic prospects of the United States vary considerably. Although supply-side economics has been discredited, conservative economics (lower taxation, less regulation, less government interference) remains alive and well. There continue to be strong efforts to reduce taxes and the role of government. On the other hand, many liberals (e.g., Robert Reich, Laura Tyson, and Clinton himself) subscribe to the "strategic trader" theory of the necessity of competing internationally.

The strategic trader analysis goes something like this: America is part of a global economy. To maintain its high standard of living, it has to compete in a tough world marketplace. That's why high productivity and product quality are essential. Competitiveness requires developing high-value sectors of the economy that will generate good jobs for the future, and this development may require selective government help (Krugman, 1992, p. 246). (Clinton's education policy similarly prescribes that American education become internationally competitive by adopting international standards of performance.)

The strategic trader position is represented by Lester Thurow, who gives the United States only a limited chance of winning the impending international competition because of its previous economic successes, consequent inertia, and lack of understanding of the problem (Gilpin, 1987; Kennedy, 1993; Thurow, 1992). "But [the United States] squandered much of its starting advantage by allowing its educational system to atrophy, by allowing itself to run a high-consumption, low-investment society, and by incurring huge international debts. No one at the end of the twentieth century is less prepared for the competition that lies ahead in the twenty-first century" (Thurow, 1992, p. 254).

To be sure, major competitors have significant problems of their own. In 1992 the average German hourly wage plus benefits was $26.90 per hour, compared with $15.89 in the United States, $19.23 in Japan, $14.70 in Spain, and $14.61 in Britain (Cohen, 1993). Germany lost manufacturing to cheaper locations overseas and had reduced its R&D investment to 2.58% of GDP in 1994, lower than current U.S. and Japanese rates (Bering, 1993). And Japan has problems with an entrenched bureaucracy, an archaic distribution system, and a huge trade surplus.

However, Paul Krugman, a leading trade economist, believes the international competitiveness argument is seriously misconstrued.

> It is simply not the case that the world's leading nations are to any important degree in economic competition with each other, or that any of their major economic problems can be attributed to failures to compete on world markets. (Krugman, 1994a, p. 30)

In his analysis, international trade is not a zero-sum game (though international status and power certainly depend on economic growth). The political urge to reduce economic problems to those of global trade competition deflects attention from the real concern—improving productivity domestically, especially in the service sectors (such as education). Ninety percent of the American economy is domestic. By overemphasizing foreign competition, bad policies result, for example, supporting only research that can improve competitiveness or focusing on manufacturing to the exclusion of the service sector, which lags in productivity. Of course, blaming the Japanese is popular; what may be bad economics is good politics.

> The roots of inadequate productivity performance are deep and poorly understood; the causes of growing inequality and poverty hardly less so. If the President insists on finding advisers willing to claim that they can solve these problems, he will inevitably find himself listening to men and women whose certainty is based on ignorance. (Krugman, 1994b, p. 283)

According to Krugman (1992), the three most important factors for the standard of living are productivity, income distribution, and unemployment. The trade deficit and inflation are secondary, except where they affect the other three. The things that can be done about productivity are to raise the quantity and quality of business capital (e.g., the savings rate); improve public capital that supports the private economy (e.g., research and infrastructure investment); and improve the work force (better education). In fact, productivity improved 2.8% in 1992, a significant increase (Krugman, 1994b, p. 129).

Most agree that serious economic reform requires hard choices among consumption, investment, and defense. The end of the Cold War allowed the possibility of reducing defense spending, but defense spending has declined less than expected. Clinton's original plan was to cut the $273 billion defense budget by 30% by 1997, though it was doubtful he would be able to manage this much against congressional opposition (Silk, 1992). In 1993 the defense budget was $297.6 (*Economist*, 1995). Defense spending is likely to remain high.

To increase investment, the United States must repay its national debt and tolerate a significant decline in its standard of living. It must reverse its productivity decline and rebuild exports by accelerating domestic investment (Gilpin, 1987). However, an extended decline in the standard of living can undermine political stability and result in protectionist pressures, evident in the campaigns of Ross Perot and Patrick Buchanan.

Inaction is not an American trait. Americans are too impatient, their expectations too high, to accept a long decline in their standard of living gracefully, as the British have done. A virulent populism and deep-seated distrust of government can still be awakened in the population. Furthermore, American populism contains strong elements of nativism and xenophobia. Hostility is likely to be directed at the establishment, the government, immigrants, minorities, and foreign powers.

The difficulty of economic reform is evidenced by Clinton's problems in passing his first budget aimed at reducing the federal deficit. Republicans refused to raise taxes on the wealthy, and Democrats refused to vote for modest sacrifices. The difference between an acceptable and an unacceptable higher gasoline tax in the budget was $1.18 per driver per month—not the choice of a people ready to sacrifice. This reluctance to sacrifice for investment is reinforced by a robust consumer culture.

In some ways the United States is facing complex economic trends that Britain encountered decades ago—global financialization, lower productivity, heavy debt, inability to reduce military spending, increasing social stratification, and economic polarization. Since 1970 Britain has lost 50% of its manufacturing jobs, compared with losses of 8% in the United States, 18% in France, and 17% in Germany, and a gain of 20% in Japan (*Economist*, 1994b). Barberis and May (1993) point out that the British decline was only *relative* to overwhelming economic dominance at one time. Although Britain went from 4th to 12th in income per capita from 1953 to the mid-1980s, income was higher in absolute terms.

During the decline, decisions by individual British firms to invest for higher profits abroad did not serve the country as a whole, which needed investment at home. Britain's class structure impeded the entrepreneurialism of its managers and the flexibility of manager and worker relations. Some contend that the British establishment harbored an antibusiness attitude, fostered by the educational system of public schools and ancient universities (education at fault again).

Politically, various interests became institutionalized so that large-scale change was difficult. These institutions included global militarism, the dominance of financial institutions, and a free trade establishment. There was no single, simple explanation for Britain's (relative) decline. Similarly, Krugman (1994b) put the matter of America's declining productivity this way:

> Why did the magic economy go away? Hundreds of books have been written on that topic. . . . The real answer is that we don't know. There are a lot of stories out there . . . most of them are dead wrong on logical or factual grounds . . . but if you are honest with yourself, you will admit that nobody, yourself included, knows which if any of these stories actually is true. (p. 5)

Such an equivocal economic analysis is not likely to inspire politicians looking for campaign issues. For whatever reasons, the economy declined, and the decline resulted in dramatic shifts in social and educational policies. Even though education had little to do with most causes of the decline, it was blamed nonetheless.

## THE ROLE OF EDUCATION

The liberal view of the relationship between education and the economy has been stated somewhat technically by Berlin and Sum (1988):

> Achievement (basic skills) determines attainment (number of years of schooling completed), which then determines employability and earnings, which influences the likelihood of marrying and bearing children within a two-parent family. Thus, there is a strong relationship between low basic skills and the incidence of welfare dependency among young adults. . . . More to the point, when other factors are controlled for, basic skill levels are an independent determinant of earnings and antisocial behavior. (pp. 28, 35)

This is an argument for *more* education, which will lead to individual and social improvement. About the same time, conservatives and neoconservatives (Bloom, 1987; Hirsch, 1987; Murray, 1984; Ravitch & Finn, 1987) declared that education had gone off course in what was taught, thus causing social and economic problems. More discipline, more rigor, higher standards, instruction in values, and cultural literacy were needed. This is an argument for *different*, rather than more, education. In my opinion, neither of these views is quite correct—that education is the prime driver of the economy, or that poor education has resulted in a declining economy.

Some economists contend that the new "information age" economy is based on a deeper penetration of science, technology, labor skills, and managerial knowledge into production processes (Castells, 1993). The more complex the economy, the more information is required. Success in international competition therefore depends on technological capacity, access to a large expanding market, and the ability of national institutions to guide the growth process. Hence, investment in human resources, especially education and information networks, is necessary, as well as strong guidance by the government (Carnoy, 1993).

So if a country is declining economically (relatively), it should invest more in its education system to improve productivity, according to this analysis. If education is mismatched to work, then it should be transformed. Yet this is not what has been happening in the United States. Rather, education is being reduced in size, autonomy, and costs. Educational reforms are not following work-place reforms, such as the teamwork required by the new production processes, devolving decision making to those closer to the work, or improving individual problem solving capacity (Carnoy & Levin, 1985).

Rather, educational resources are being reduced. In the 1950s education expenditures per K–12 student increased 44%, 69% in the 1960s, 35% in the 1970s, and 33% in the 1980s (Odden & Massy, 1992). In the 1990s, however, prospects were bleak. "Whatever the reason or reasons for it, the rise in education spending was short-lived. By 1991–92, state expenditures for education were not keeping up with inflation. Similarly, local support barely kept up with inflation after 1989–90" (Educational Commission of the States, 1993, p. iv). One reason for declining state spending was that the federal government forced costs onto states because of its own budget problems.

Also, there has been a public perception that not much has been gained for increased expenditures. The extra money went to increased teacher salaries, more course offerings, support services, higher administrative costs, and reductions in class size (Odden & Massy, 1992). About 60% of each education dollar is used for direct classroom instruction. A leading business journal expressed strong opposition to increased educational spending:

> Spending on education has increased as wealth has grown. . . . Education . . . is acting not like a necessity but like a luxury. At least in part it seems to function not as an investment good but as a consumption good. Which means that spending on education is no more sacrosanct than spending on whiskey. The educational establishment's sanctimoniousness might be excusable if the educators could point to results from this increased spending. But the statistics all show a catastrophic and continuing productivity decline. Annual current expenditure per pupil . . . has virtually quadrupled since 1949. . . . US education is in essence a socialized business, the American equivalent of the Soviet Union's collectivized farm. (*Forbes Magazine*, 1986, pp. 75, 76)

Conceiving education as private consumption rather than public investment is a significant turn away from the policies of the liberal period. It signifies that education is not primarily a public responsibility, but a private good, meant to profit the individual and not deserving of more public investment. It may be that the relationship between education and the economy is changing or, perhaps, that it never was the way it has been popularly conceived.

Human capital theorists see the connection between education and the economy as complex. From 1900 to 1940 the rates of return on college and high school education declined. After 1940 the rates of return either increased or did not decline, presumably because of the growth of expenditures on R&D and military technology (Becker, 1993). The gap between high school and college earnings was stable until the 1960s, fell in the 1970s, then rose sharply during the 1980s and 1990s. Gary Becker (1993), a leading human capital economist, suggested:

> In the United States during much of the last eighty years, a narrowing of wage ratios has gone hand in hand with an increasing relative supply of skill, an association that is usually said to result from the effect of an autonomous increase in the supply of skills—brought about by the spread of free education or the rise in incomes—on the return to skill, as measured by wage ratios. An alternative interpretation suggested by the analysis here is that the spread of education and the increased investment in other kinds of human capital were in large part *induced* by technological progress (and perhaps other changes) through the effect on the rate of return, as measured by wage differences and costs. (p. 90)

In other words, in the traditional view, lower wages may occur because of more skilled workers, or because of competition with workers in other countries. In Becker's (1993) view, schooling raises earnings and productivity by providing knowledge and skills, but these increases depend on the jobs available. People acquire education when they anticipate that it will have payoffs.

Presumably in modern economies these jobs depend on the expansion of scientific and technological knowledge, which improves production processes. This knowledge is embodied in people through schooling and on-the-job training. In a sense the need for education is dependent on job technology. For example, traditional farmers have no need for formal education since their traditional technology can be passed on from parents to children. On the other hand, modern farmers do need formal training and do acquire it.

Some economists believe that the increase in schooling from 1929 to 1982 "explains" (statistically) about one-fourth of the rise in per capita income during this period, with some of the "unaccounted for" increase being due to the difficulty of measuring improvements in health, on-the-job training, and other forms of human capital investment. Part of the rapid industrial development of the "Asian tiger" countries is due to the presence of an educated, hard-working, conscientious work force. The Japanese also invested heavily in formal education and on-the-job training. Their lifetime system of employment is explained not simply by Japanese culture, but by the investment the companies make in employee training, an investment too expensive to abandon. In the early half of the century, job changes were frequent in Japan.

Although formal education has been greatly emphasized, on-the-job training has been underemphasized. Most workers increase their productivity by learning new skills on the job. Some knowledge acquired this way is *general* knowledge, which can be applied any place the person works, and some is *specific* knowledge, applicable only in the organization the person is working for. Employers typically pay those with specific knowledge more than those with general knowledge because these employees are the ones the firm can least afford to lose. Quit and layoff rates are inversely related to the amount and cost of "specific" job training because both firm and employee want to protect their specific investments (see discussion in Becker, 1993, pp. 30–51).

This point is critical to my argument for how to improve the productivity of schools, presented in Part II of this book. The concept of specific, on-the-job learning applies especially to teachers as employees. Teachers have both general and specific knowledge, the latter one of the most overlooked features of their work. Teachers learn how to teach mostly on the job, though a considerable amount of general information—subject-matter knowledge—can be learned formally in school. During a few years on the job, teachers acquire specialized knowledge about individual students and develop special skills. These skills constitute a significant investment by the teacher and the school.

This specific investment causes teachers to behave differently than school reformers expect them to behave. In fact, their behavior is explained by "transaction cost" economics. In Part II, I will develop these ideas as an explanation of critical factors that school reform policies overlook. In brief, teachers have a significant investment in the specific skills and knowledge they have acquired, and they protect their professional investments. School reform policies must take these human capital investments into account at risk of failure.

## EDUCATION AND THE ECONOMY: A CHANGING RELATIONSHIP?

Education is tied closely to the modern economy. As long as we have a technological economy that requires highly educated workers, there is a need for formal education. An educated work force is needed to implement the ideas and technologies generated by R&D. Both R&D and education are factors of production. However, this interdependent relationship may change, as it has in the past. For one thing, informal education may play a larger role through television, the Internet, and new media possibilities.

For example, Levin (1993a) challenges the view that jobs at the turn of the century will require considerably more education. So far, only about 5% of workers are in jobs that require substantial worker decisions, autonomy, and training. Rather, the tendency has been to hire "disposable workers," who work part-time or on contract. Such jobs have increased to half of all new employment. The 10 fastest growing job categories do require considerable education. However, by far the largest total number of jobs exist at the lower end of the scale. Jobs that require a high school education or less will shrink to only 46% from 48% of the total by the year 2000. The need for college graduates will increase from 21% in 1986 to only 23% by the year 2000.

Although the gap in wages between college and high school graduates has increased substantially, wages for males of both groups fell between 1968 and 1987. Wages for high school graduates have simply fallen faster. The wages of college-educated white males, 45–54 years old, fell 17% between 1986 and 1992, partly as a result of "downsizing" by corporations. Falling wages is a new phenomenon for the college educated, though it happened earlier in the century (Uchitelle, 1994). One out of five college graduates has a job that does not require a college degree (Levin, 1993a).

There is another, darker possibility. In the 1970s many American multinational corporations became more foreign investors in other countries than domestic producers who export. Some major corporations have more than half their assets and earnings overseas. By the 1980s some corporations were importing their newest developments from abroad. In an era in which corporations can invest capital, manufacture, and sell goods in almost any part of the world, how expensive an education system need they support in their home country? It may pay them to move operations where they can find cheap labor, even educated labor.

So far, labor competition with foreign workers has been limited to manufacturing jobs and credited with keeping wage inflation under control. Service jobs are more difficult to move, though not impossible. What is to prevent competition at higher job levels? Good engineers are available in many places in the world. Experienced computer programmers in the United States earn $4,000 to $6,000 per month, compared with $1,200 to $1,500 per month in India. American companies have moved tens of thousands of programming jobs to Asia, the work from which can be beamed back to the United States overnight (Bradsher, 1995).

A permanent retrenchment in education may be beginning, similar to what happened in Britain under Thatcher and Major (Kogan & Kogan, 1983). Britain has an older economy in which global financialization, the investment of capital overseas where it earns a better rate of return, led to deterioration of domestic industry decades ago. British retrenchment in higher education resulted in reduced funding, transformed governance, loss of tenure, and the flight of academics.

Cheaper labor has been a pursuit of American business, whether through increasing immigration, relocating manufacturing plants, or taking advantage of labor markets segmented by race, gender, and ethnicity (Bergmann, 1986). Cheaper labor might mean reducing the education of workers rather than improving it, especially when there are not enough jobs for the educated. In fact, lack of jobs for the educated calls the legitimacy of the entire social system into question.

Of course, such a scenario is partly compensated for by the fact that the social rates of return on educational investment outweigh the private rates of return. Hence, education might be subsidized by the state beyond its benefits to the economy. However, social returns decrease the greater the income of the country (and aggregate spending on education). Poorer countries get a higher return from their education investment ("Investing in people," 1994). Also, there is a higher return from primary education than secondary, and from secondary than higher education (research excluded).

There is also a disjuncture between what many reformers want the schools to do and what business and industry want. Most reformers and media focus on achievement as represented by standardized tests. Yet these hardly reflect business concerns.

> Economists have long been aware that conventional measures of ability—intelligence tests or aptitude scores, school grades, and personality tests—while undoubtedly relevant at times, do not reliably measure the talents needed to succeed in the economic sphere. The latter consists of particular kinds of personality, persistence, and intelligence. (Becker, 1993, p. 97)

The strong push for higher test scores is surprising in that achievement test scores account for only about 6% of the statistical variance in supervisor work ratings (Levin, 1993a). A one-standard deviation increase in test scores, a large change, makes for only a 7 to 15% difference in wages, a significant but not huge difference. A male in the 84th percentile in math in 1986 earns about 8% *less* than one at the 16th percentile in 1978. Achievement conventionally understood accounts for less in the economic world than most people assume, including those who write national reports blaming industrial decline on the schools.

Perhaps that is why businesses stress different student outcomes. In a recent survey employers expressed little confidence in the schools' ability to prepare students for jobs. In selecting students for jobs, employers disregarded grades and test scores in favor of attitudes and work experience. Attitude, communication skills, and previous work experience were the most important traits sought, while test scores placed 8th out of 11 (Applebome, 1995).

In this same survey employers expressed considerable hostility toward young workers. A researcher said, "In the focus groups the response was scatological." None of the employers provided remedial training for their workers. Such data raise questions about what the schools are teaching in relation to work (Wirth, 1992). Levin (1993b) asserts that the schools should be teaching for broader goals, initiative, cooperation, working in peer groups, evaluation, communication, reasoning, problem solving, and decision making, while business puts character traits high on the list.

The social dislocation caused by unemployment, shifting employment, and individuals moving countrywide to seek jobs, unmoored from their extended families, local communities, and churches—the traditional sources of norms of conduct—results in schools' taking blame and responsibility for character traits developed largely outside their control. The source of these problems resides more in unintentional effects from the economic structure itself.

## CONCLUSION

The United States faces a serious economic productivity problem. Its productivity rate has declined over the past several decades, which translates into a lower standard of living, or more work for the same standard of living. There are several reasons for this, including lack of investment in R&D, the American style of short-term business management, bureaucratization of large firms, and slowness in adopting revolutionary production techniques. However, no economist fully understands why productivity has declined or how to remedy it, though all point to relevant factors. Although "strategic traders" and "supply side" advocates contend that solutions lie in improving international competitiveness or cutting taxes and regulations, much of the problem seems to lie in domestic service sectors of the economy.

Similarly, I doubt that the productivity problems in American education—and how to improve education—have much to do with what other countries are doing. The real problem is to increase the productivity of American schools by focusing on how teaching and learning are organized. Worrying about foreign competition in education may lead to bad policy in the same way it does for the strategic traders. Improving education that fits the United States and American culture is the better course. Of course, one might learn from other countries, but imitation is usually based on a misunderstanding of the foreign country itself.

Furthermore, education's role in the economy is much more complex than popularly presented. The idea that education leads to a better job and economy is too simple. The technology of jobs requires certain kinds of knowledge, and people learn this knowledge when the jobs are there to be had. In a sense, the jobs often precede the education. Also, on-the-job learning is greatly underestimated as contributing to improved productivity, and this is especially true for teaching.

A look into the near future indicates that many jobs will not require more education, and that corporations might reasonably import educated workers or place jobs in other countries where the workers already have a high degree of education. Supporting an expensive education system at home may not be in their interest. There is also a disjuncture between traditional achievement and the character traits that many in business say they want in students. It is possible that the role of education in the economy is changing or that it never was the way it is popularly portrayed.

# CHAPTER 5

# REINVENTING GOVERNMENT

To complete the conceptual structure delineating relationships between education and the economy, I want to deal with the fourth relationship—how concepts and metaphors from economics and business penetrate government policy. In this chapter the topic is Clinton and Gore's attempt to reform the entire federal government structure based on market concepts. First, I identify the sources of the reform ideas, how they were implemented in government policy, what the results are so far, and what the deeper problems are in general with the application of such ideas to government, including a discussion of "imperfect" markets in government contracting.

When somewhat idealized reform ideas—idealized because they are presumed to be business practices—are employed in the public sector, two things must be kept in mind. First, many of the ideas have never been implemented in business the way they are presented. Second, the public sector is different from the private sector in many ways, and one cannot always apply the ideas in the same way. One must make adjustments. The point is not to abandon such efforts, but to apply the ideas with some caution. Too often they are applied uncritically.

## SOURCES OF "REINVENTING GOVERNMENT"

Perhaps the most distinctive characteristic of the Clinton administration is "reinventing government." Ordinarily liberals want to use government to solve social problems, while conservatives want less government and want problems to be solved through the private sector. This has been the major issue distinguishing Democrats from Republicans since Roosevelt's New Deal. Clinton and Gore saw themselves as "neoliberals" who wanted a strong role for government in solving social problems, but a different role. Government itself had to be transformed so that it became more effective, efficient, and entrepreneurial—more like business.

Clinton's major attempt to reform the federal bureaucracy was based on a set of ideas about entrepreneurial activity put together by a journalist and the mayor of a small town. These were not ideas advanced by an established economist. Rather, the ideas gained currency through policy entrepreneurs, much like supply-side economics in the Reagan administration. Similar ideas have been advanced in other countries, for example, Britain, Australia, and New Zealand (Boston et al., 1996; Kelsey, 1995; Pusey, 1991).

The reinventing-government campaign was launched by Vice-President Gore a few months after the Clinton administration took office. As Gore (1993) noted, "only 20 percent of Americans trust the federal government to do the right thing most of the time—down from 76 percent twenty years ago" (p. xxix). Five of six people want fundamental change in Washington. By making government more responsive, trust in government might be restored. Government could still be made to work successfully, if properly reformed.

The basic idea was that old-fashioned government consisted of large bureaucracies that provided valuable services but eventually became inflexible and indifferent to their clients. Government had to find new ways of addressing social problems, often by adopting techniques pioneered in business, even while recognizing that government is different from business: Government serves the public interest while business serves private interests.

Osborne and Gaebler's *Reinventing Government* (1992) was the major source of these ideas, which were applied to the federal government in *Creating a Government That Works Better and Costs Less* (Gore, 1993). From this perspective centralized bureaucracies become preoccupied with rules and regulations, encumbered with hierarchical chains of command, and no longer function well because they have become bloated, wasteful, and impersonal. American business corporations exhibited similar deficiencies in past decades, but in the 1980s businesses decentralized authority, flattened hierarchies, and focused on quality and customers, resulting in better performance. Governments should become more entrepreneurial.

> Most entrepreneurial governments promote *competition* between service providers. They *empower* citizens by pushing control out of the bureaucracy, into the community. They measure the performance of their agencies, focusing not on inputs but on *outcomes*. They are driven by their goals—their *missions*—not by their rules and regulations. They redefine their clients as *customers* and offer them choices . . . . They *prevent* problems before they emerge, rather than simply offering services afterward. They put their energies into *earning* money, not simply spending it. They *decentralize* authority, embracing participatory management. They prefer *market* mechanisms to bureaucratic mechanisms. And they focus on *catalyzing* all sectors—public, private, voluntary—into action to solve their community's problems. (Osborne & Gaebler, 1992, pp. 19–20, emphasis in original)

Entrepreneurial government "steers" rather than "rows," that is, guides rather than produces services. Governments can act as catalysts by bringing together public, nonprofit, and profit-making organizations to address public problems, letting others do the work while government guides the services. Governments may also promote competition among government units, such as by having garbage collection units bid against private companies for contracts. Competition is a key concept. Noncompetitive private service providers are as inefficient as noncompetitive public monopolies, in Osborne and Gaebler's (1992) view.

Procurement and outsourcing government services are two major ways of promoting competition. However, in order for contracting to work, the bidding must be truly competitive, based on "hard" information about cost and quality of performance, monitored carefully, and a nonpolitical body established to perform such tasks. Another important strategy is to clarify the organizational mission, so that people are not lost in the maze of rules and regulations established at one time to control corruption but that now impede action.

Funding on the basis of outcomes rather than inputs is another key idea. "Performance indicators" can provide specific measures of service quality for each government unit. Customer satisfaction is a performance indicator recommended for government services, including schools. One might define the recipients of services as "customers" and focus on their satisfaction, as in Total Quality Management (TQM). In one highly praised TQM implementation at Fox Valley Technical College, Wisconsin, the customers were identified as students, employers, and the community.

Another area for improvement is preventing problems rather than solving them after they emerge. The Environmental Protection Agency spends most of its budget trying to clean up pollution rather than preventing it. And even though the United States has by far the most expensive medical system in the world, it ranks 20th in infant mortality, partly through failure to provide preventive care. Decentralization is another favorite strategy that promotes responsive government, encourages innovation, and generates higher morale and flexibility. The Tactical Air Command transformed itself into an effective organization through radical decentralization. Participatory management, employee involvement, and training are integral parts of decentralization.

Another strategy is for government to create markets in order to make bureaucracies more market-oriented. This is in preference to program provision, which tends to be driven by political constituencies rather than by customers and to result in fragmented services and programs whose turf must be defended. Such service programs are not self-correcting, rarely die, and rely on commands (rules and regulations) rather than incentives. The worst examples of "command" programs, according to Osborne and Gaebler (1992), were the top-down educational reforms of the 1980s, in which states ordered compliance with rules and regulations. This engendered resistance and poor results. Creating incentives through markets is a better idea.

Putting all these strategies together for education, Osborne and Gaebler (1992) recommend having state and local school boards set minimum standards, measure performance, enforce equity goals, and provide financing, but have the schools run on a contract or voucher basis by different organizations, such as teacher groups, colleges, or community organizations, rather than being operated by school districts. In other words, local governments would guide rather than produce services. Each school would manage itself, while the state would measure and publicize results, including test scores; student work; parent, teacher, and student satisfaction; dropout rates; college placement rates; observations by experts; and honors won by students.

The primary "customers," the parents, could use such information to choose schools for their children; incentives would replace commands. "The problem with education is not that we don't know what works. We do. The research is clear, and there is remarkable consensus among education specialists. The problem is that many schools won't—or can't—do what works. . . . *No one has to change. No one has to do better*" (Osborne & Gaebler, 1992, p. 318, emphasis in original). In their view, incentives would induce schools to improve and shake them from their lethargy. (One might note that consensus on what works in schools is considerably more contentious than the authors suggest.)

Many of these strategies may conflict with one another, depending on how they are employed. For example, focusing on a centrally defined mission and concentrating on improving customer satisfaction can lead in different directions. Also, measures of educational outcomes are not the same as measures of customer satisfaction. Nor is decentralization the same as centrally defined missions. The reinventing-government platform is eclectic, which doesn't mean it can't be effective. Often, eclecticism works better in the real world than does pure theory. But the suggested reform strategies are not tied together in a tightly reasoned way.

## APPLIED TO THE FEDERAL GOVERNMENT

The National Performance Review (NPR) (Gore, 1993) applied several of these ideas to the federal government. The review was conducted by a team of senior federal bureaucrats who identified obstacles blocking effective government action. The report itself is admirably frank in assessing bureaucratic deficiencies. Reform concepts from the report include measuring results, "putting the customer in the driver's seat," introducing competition and market orientation, and decentralizing (Gore, 1993, p. xii).

Specific recommendations include reducing the civilian work force by 12% over 5 years, with reductions focused on "control" personnel such as auditors and procurement specialists, whose regulations make action difficult. Control personnel constitute one-third of federal employees, or 700,000 people; there is one manager for every seven employees in the government. Other recommendations are aimed at reducing procedures that were introduced originally to control fraud and spending, but that make operations inefficient. Allowing employees more discretion in their jobs is central.

The report recognizes the fragmentation of federal programs. There are 340 separate programs for families and children, administered by 11 different agencies, spending about $60 billion a year, but little connection among them. I have already discussed the hundreds of mathematics and science education programs funded by a dozen different departments and agencies, with little coordination among them.

According to the NPR report, government employees, especially those at lower grades, lack training opportunities. They operate with outmoded equipment; many are alienated and unmotivated. Recommendations range from finding a new mission for the Department of Energy (making nuclear weapons is on hold) to reducing the number of Department of Education programs from 230 to 189. President Clinton also ordered federal executive agencies to identify "customers," survey the customers to determine what services they want, establish standards and measure results, "benchmark" the standards to business, and report results to the president (Executive Order, September 11, 1993).

Independent of reinventing government but complementary to it, the Congressional Government Performance and Results Act of 1993 (Public Law 103-62) required federal agencies to develop measures of progress by which their performance can be evaluated. Declaring that "waste and inefficiency in Federal programs undermine the confidence of the American people in the Government and reduce the Federal Government's ability to address adequately public needs," Congress mandated that by 1997 the head of each federal agency submit a strategic plan for program activities to the Office of Management and Budget (OMB). This plan had to include mission, goals and objectives, and description of operational processes.

By law, the Office of Management and Budget must require every federal agency to express its goals in "objective, quantifiable, and measurable" form and establish performance indicators to measure outputs and outcomes, unless OMB specifically approves an alternative form. There was provision for qualitative measures in some cases. This evaluation must be based on whether the goals are achieved, and by the year 2000 these agencies must report results. OMB also designated 10 agencies to conduct pilot projects in 1994–1996 with assessment of projects by 1997.

## AN ASSESSMENT OF REINVENTING GOVERNMENT

Whether these sweeping reforms can be accomplished is a good question. Every administration tries to reform the bureaucracy and promises to reduce costs, but few lasting changes occur. Somehow the changes tend to be cosmetic and the bureaucracy lumbers on. The hierarchical nature of bureaucracy in which decisions have to be approved at several higher levels creates many of the problems of inefficiency. Yet this same hierarchy is supposed to institute the reforms, thus reducing the power of those in high places and empowering those below.

Although the NPR is frank about the difficulties of instituting reforms, can one expect the hierarchy to reform itself? Cynics would say that experienced bureaucrats might be expected to hunker down, knowing that this initiative will pass with the Clinton administration. Although the goals are admirable, a carefully thought out strategy for implementation is needed to institute changes, and such an implementation strategy is not spelled out in the report.

A few years after the National Performance Review was launched, Kettl (1994, 1995), a leading expert on government contracting, and others (Ban, 1995; Radin, 1995) conducted an early assessment of its progress. As public relations the reform effort was an immediate success, with Clinton's approval ratings jumping 12 percentage points. However, within 2 months the effort began to stall (DiIulio, 1995). First, pressure from Congress for quick results led officials to shrink the number of personnel first, delaying other important operational reforms. Furthermore, the personnel cuts (272,900) were at the middle-manager level, which alienated many government workers.

Actually, most of the problems with the excessive federal hierarchy are with the 3,000 political appointees, who form layers through which actions must pass for approval. These layers were unaffected by the reform. Therefore many career bureaucrats did not sign on to the project and began to regard it as one more rhetorical reform that would pass away. "Faced with a choice of taking large risks toward uncertain ends or riding out the storm in an admittedly leaky boat, many managers chose to take the conservative course" (Kettl, 1994, p. 61).

Second, there was no explicit strategy for dealing with Congress, without whose support no serious reform was possible. Congress immediately exempted the Veteran's Health Administration from cuts, then criminal justice activities. In a sense the NPR attempts to shift power from Congress to the bureaucracy and from the top levels of the bureaucracy to the bottom levels. However, not surprisingly, congressional factions continued to protect their constituencies. The administration could sustain none of the recommendations without congressional support (Kettl, 1994), and traditionally Congress has been more concerned with distribution than with efficiency (Foreman, 1995).

Since each federal department was free to proceed on its own, different things occurred in each. In the Department of Agriculture, for example, career bureaucrats emphasized empowerment of managers and changes in decision processes, while political appointees were interested in policy changes, reorganization, and budget reductions. Almost all efforts across departments adopted concepts, models, and expertise from the private sector (Radin, 1995).

Some critics contended that the NPR effort was an internally contradictory ensemble of ideas based on three different reform strategies: "downsizing," "reengineering," and "continuous improvement." Downsizing means simply to shrink the public sector. "One principle has guided it: the only way to force greater efficiency is to put a cocked gun, in the form of tax and spending limits, to the heads of public managers" (Kettl, 1995, p. 39). Reengineering requires fundamental changes in the work process itself, while continuous improvement strives to improve things slowly, often through changes in interpersonal relations, for example, giving consumers a voice and choice. These lead in different directions.

One can see how these internal contradictions play out in practice with the function of evaluation. Both reinventing government and the Congressional Government Performance and Results Act rely heavily on assessment of the results of government agency programs. In fact, Kettl (1995) suggests that performance measurement is one of three critical things that must be done to salvage the effort. Yet in 1994 executive branch evaluation offices found their authority to conduct evaluations unchanged (71%) or decreased (21%), and their funding the same (43%) or decreased (36%), in spite of greater evaluation responsibilities (Wargo, 1994). As one observer suggested, "It is not easy to link policy and management agendas" (Radin, 1995, p. 130).

After two years, experts on reinventing government thought the movement not self-sustaining—unless revitalization took place somehow. "Successful reinvention requires linking the big-politics of downsizing with the small-politics of performance improvement" (Kettl, 1994, p. 58), but there was little evidence that this was occurring. Also, the Clinton administration had to deal with the new Republican Congress and its intensely negative attitude toward the federal bureaucracy (Foreman, 1995). For some critics reinventing government was one more chapter in the historic conflict between the Hamiltonians, who want to increase the effectiveness of executive power, and the Madisonians, who want checks and balances against the executive (Garvey, 1995). The Madisonians seemed to be winning.

## PROBLEMS WITH MARKET POLICIES

The idea of using private enterprise to conduct public business is not new. Every major policy initiative of the federal government since World War II has been managed through public-private partnerships, whether it be Medicare, manufacture of nuclear weapons, antipoverty programs, space programs, or interstate highways (Kettl, 1993). The pace of such activities increased in the 1970s when the federal work force declined. By FY1991 federal outlays for contracts amounted to $210 billion out of $1.4 trillion total federal spending. In fact, the most egregious examples of waste and fraud have been committed by the government's private partners, such as defense contractors. So the establishment of entrepreneurial government does not in itself ensure effective management.

In public-private partnerships, contracts replace hierarchy as a way of getting the job done. Instead of a chain of command there is a negotiated document that separates the policymaker from policy output. (The National Performance Review even recommended that the president draw up a contract with his department heads as the basis for management.) The government must write a contract that induces the contractor to behave as the government wants. Of course, contractors always have their own interests to pursue, which are not identical to the public interest. Furthermore, the government must monitor the contract to ensure compliance. Goals must be defined in advance to provide guidance for the contractual relationship.

> The new element is not "consumer sovereignty," however, nor greater rights for individuals. Rather, it is the fact that the parties to the contract have separate interests. In this sense, "competition" is inherent in the contractual approach; not competition between different purchasers, or different providers of services, but in the contractual relationship itself. The public interest—i.e. the overall functioning of the public service in question—is not the responsibility of a single unitary organization, but instead emerges from the process of agreement between separate organizations, none of which has responsibility for the public interest as a whole. (Harden, 1992, p. 33)

A competitive market presumes there are many competent contractors who can do the job. Often there is only one or a few. Defining the product desired is no easy task, especially if the task is complicated. The difficulty of task specification induces the government and the contractor to work together cooperatively, thus violating or compromising an arm's-length relationship. Of course, bureaucratic politics also intrudes into market relationships since it is critical for bureaucracies to build political constituencies. Many decisions are made with an eye toward strengthening political positions. The common idea of a competitive market doesn't always work as one might expect.

For example, in the past decade, Congress has given the National Science Foundation $600 million for science education and has been insistent that the programs purchased with this money be evaluated. The evaluation office has a small staff of three and one-half evaluators who contract out more than $12 million in evaluations each year. The studies are done mostly by private firms located in Washington (House, 1995; House, Haug, & Norris, 1996).

The neoclassical conception of a competitive market is something like this: There are many buyers and sellers of goods and services, and these buyers and sellers operate at arm's length. No single buyer or seller can dominate the market. Goods are undifferentiated so that there is no overwhelming advantage of buying from a particular seller. Sellers have incentives to produce goods and services at the lowest competitive price, or the buyer can go to another seller.

Similarly, sellers can go to other buyers if they are not getting a fair price for their products. In neoclassical markets, faceless buyers and sellers meet to exchange standardized goods at equilibrium prices. An open market is a contractual situation in which there is a uniform price available to all comers impersonally. Competition among buyers and sellers keeps prices low and product quality high, leading to efficiency in the production of a particular good or service (Kettl, 1993). In many instances this neoclassical market seems to work fairly well.

However, this is not what we have in the evaluation market. There are only a few buyers—the government agencies. Even in a government as large as that of the United States, there are relatively few agencies that contract out evaluations. So the market is imperfect on the demand (government) side. More surprisingly, the market is also imperfect on the supply (contractor) side. Typically, only a few firms bid for contracts. In the NSF office, four firms do almost all the evaluation contracting. How can this be?

Over a period of time the evaluation firms tend to become specialized in the evaluations they do. The more successful firms can afford to hire personnel for long periods of time, even when they do not have contracts. Small firms can ill afford to be unemployed for long. Over time the larger firms tend to drive out the smaller ones, whom they may hire as subcontractors. Furthermore, the larger firms become highly specialized through their contacts with government agencies. The same firms win NSF contracts year after year and keep on staff people who specialize in science education evaluation.

The firms deal with the same government people. They get to know evaluation and program personnel inside NSF. They come to know what NSF likes. In almost all cases successful firms maintain offices in Washington. They establish professional and personal friendships by attending the same meetings. In some cases agency and firm employees socialize together. There is much personal contact back and forth in the normal negotiating, supervising, and monitoring of contracts.

For their part, the NSF staff discovers who is dependable. They find out which individuals in the firms are trustworthy, who will do a good job and who won't. Sometimes it happens that the contracting firm hires someone who doesn't do a good job. The government doesn't ordinarily go to another contractor. Rather, after some haggling, the government officer will call a supervisor within the firm and say that the unfortunate person should be replaced on the contract.

Since the firm depends heavily, though not exclusively, on this particular agency for a large portion of its funding, the firm replaces the worker at government request, a change handled informally most of the time. The NSF office can involve the legal government contracts office by formally invoking failure to discharge the contract but this strategy is not satisfactory, except in extreme cases. The legal delays are long, lawyers are involved at considerable expense, and the special relationship between the firm and the agency is injured. Formal sanction occurs but the breach must be large and serious not to be resolved by informal negotiations.

Over a period of time both sides gain special knowledge and skills from these interactions. This knowledge is very specific to the situation—the actual firms, personalities, procedures, type of work, and so on. One might call this special knowledge and skill a "specific asset," because it is an investment of sorts. Of course, knowing how to conduct evaluations is knowledge too, but more general knowledge. This special knowledge takes time to develop and it usually pays off.

If another firm tried to break into evaluation contracting at NSF, they would lack critical information about how things work, no matter their knowledge of evaluation. They might spend quite a lot of money preparing a proposal to do an evaluation without much confidence that they will win the award. And that is what happens. Four firms do most of the evaluation work for NSF in spite of the fact that bids must be let publicly, according to a lengthy set of government rules and regulations. NSF has recognized that they do business with the same firms all the time, and although the agency is happy with their contractors, they have solicited other bidders, but with limited success.

So instead of an autonomous, impersonal market of many buyers and sellers, the evaluation market consists of a set of bilateral associations between the government and firms, based on specific, personal, interdependent interactions over a long period of time, what some might call an "imperfect" market from a neoclassical view.

## IMPERFECT MARKETS

Market advocates argue that markets will discipline the public sector in the same way that they discipline the private sector. Competition can shape government services in three ways. First, the market sets the level of production by matching supply and demand. The balance between the demand of buyers and the supply of sellers establishes a production equilibrium that results in efficiency for the service produced. However, in this NSF case the demand for evaluation is set by the agency and especially by Congress's appetite for evaluation results, perhaps more for political than for economic reasons. In the NSF case there is, in essence, one buyer.

Second, markets are supposed to minimize costs because suppliers must compete with one another to underprice competitors or supply superior goods. But, in truth, whatever one may say about the positive aspects of contracting out evaluations, minimizing costs is not a result. The complex personal interactions result in more costs for contractors and the government, including the up-front costs of preparing proposals, negotiating, and so forth, and the later costs of supervising, bonding, and so forth. Sometimes these are called "transaction costs" (Williamson, 1985).

In fact, contrary to what some might think, people (and firms) with specific knowledge and skills particular to the situation will be paid *more* than those with general knowledge. Although a worker or firm with general knowledge might find work elsewhere at the prevailing market price, that person (or firm) can also be replaced at prevailing market prices, whereas the person (or firm) with job-specific knowledge and skills cannot be replaced so easily. The replacement will have to be retrained or learn the necessary specific skills on the job, increasing the cost. Both the person and the employer will be reluctant to part company because of their respective investments in each other, so that those with specific skills are paid a premium compared with what they could command on the open market (Becker, 1993).

Contracting firms and government agencies have large investments (sunk costs) in their relationships with one another. Bilateral contracting costs more than it would on an open market. Firms must have a way of recouping their costs, usually accomplished through high overhead rates. The imperfect market in defense contracting exhibits similar characteristics.

Third, the market is supposed to regulate quality by eliminating noncompetitive producers who sell inferior goods. Although the NSF contractors seem fully competent, it is not clear that inferior ones have gone out of business, though they may have. One would have to look at the market in the past to see if this has happened. In any case, the market consists of only a few firms that the government must do business with or not be able to conduct evaluations at all. Hence, the market is imperfect on the supply side as well.

When market imperfections are high, then transaction costs associated with contracted services will be high as well, especially under conditions where the government is not certain what it wants, where competition is slight, or where monitoring quality is difficult. All these apply to evaluation. The limited supply of evaluation services means that some putative advantages of contracting out (e.g., reducing bureaucratic control, cutting costs, and speeding operations) may not obtain. For example, Boston (1994) says:

> Market contracting is likely to be preferable when behavioral uncertainty is low (so that the contractor "types"—in terms of honesty, reputations and expertise—are well known and the risks of adverse selection are minimized), when the quality and quantity of the desired goods and services can be easily measured (making monitoring relatively simple and cheap), and when the number of potential suppliers is large, both during the first and subsequent contract periods. (p. 12)

In the case of evaluation contracting there is much uncertainty, the quality and quantity of services are not easily measured or easily monitored, and there are few suppliers. Interdependence with contractors is the rule, though one might regard this interdependence as an investment rather than a cost. In whichever case, it costs more than neoclassical market theory would suggest. Also, the entry cost of developing relationships with new contractors may be disproportionately high when compared with maintaining existing relationships. Both government and contractors reduce uncertainty this way. In general, the more imperfect the market, the more interdependent the government is with its contractors (Kettl, 1993).

When the market is highly imperfect on both supply and demand sides, the best the government can do is try to be a "smart buyer" of evaluation services. Being a smart buyer requires several things. First, the government agency must be able to define its goals separately from contractors so that the government knows what it wants to purchase (Kettl, 1993).

Second, the agency must know which contractors can do the job. Corporations themselves do not let blind contracts to the lowest bidder. They know better. They want someone who will do the job well and for reasonable cost. When things go wrong, the agency must know how to fix them without invoking the cumbersome legal apparatus, which would make evaluation contracting untenable. Of course, it would be better to have more contractors for competitive purposes.

Third, the agency must be able to judge what it has bought, by judging the proposal, progress, and/or the product itself. The government should be able to judge proposals and plans competently, which means there is sufficient expertise inside the agency. The problem of judging the quality of evaluation studies is more complicated than one of available expertise. Overworked resources and the necessity of government staff working closely with contractors does not make the agency staff the best judges of the finished products. One cannot provide weekly advice, engage in personal relationships, then step away and impartially judge the finished product one has helped create. Government agencies need careful procedures for judging products, possibly through a combination of outside and inside reviews.

Where market conditions are so imperfect, the organizational culture becomes extremely important because the internal culture must accomplish things that a more competitive market might achieve otherwise. Building the proper evaluation culture within the agency, among program personnel as well as evaluation staff, should be a long-term priority for agencies serious about evaluation. This means training and consulting with agency members other than evaluators.

Another critical element in any bureaucratic operation is information flow across the technical, managerial, and institutional levels that characterize large bureaucracies (Wilson, 1989). Technical workers are the ones who do the work, monitor the contracts, and run the programs. Managers, usually department and division directors, are concerned about the final products and may have only passing knowledge of contractors. Managers tend not to reward employees for their ability to monitor contracts. Institutional leaders at the top of the organization deal with legislators, the public, and other political forces to obtain resources for their agency and are only dimly aware of contracting.

Communication among these levels is problematic and can be dysfunctional.

The Challenger space shuttle "O-ring" disaster is a striking example in which technical workers (engineers) advised against the launch. The contractor, Morton Thiokol, knew the O-rings could malfunction in cold weather. Higher administrators in the National Aeronautics and Space Administration (NASA) were informed of the danger, but never fully understood the likelihood of O-ring failure. They were so concerned about the political consequences of not launching the shuttle that the disaster occurred. Since each level of the agency is concerned about different things, the chances of miscommunication are high.

Different concerns at these three levels inhibit the flow of information up and down the chain of command. To paraphrase, "Technicians see no evil. Managers speak no evil. Institutionalists hear no evil" (Kettl, 1993, pp. 189–190). In imperfect markets organizational cultures often become more important than market incentives. Information may flow across organizational channels within similar cultures.

## CONCLUSION

In the 1990s Clinton and Gore attempted to reform the federal bureaucracy within a neoliberal framework. Managerial reforms would be implemented by the executive branch, including contracting services, entrepreneurialism, performance indicators, and so forth. However, the checks and balances of the American system prevented effective implementation of these reforms. Also, the lack of a strategic plan for implementation was a serious obstacle. In the words of one astute bureaucrat, probably only several successive administrations devoted to such a reform, plus the cooperation of Congress, could implement such reforms.

However, the problems with market reforms in government run deeper than politics. Markets do not work the same way with public services as in the private sector. Few buyers and few sellers result in "imperfect markets," which function in quite a different manner than neoclassical markets with many impersonal buyers and sellers. In such imperfect markets, transaction costs are high.

One way of regarding these reforms is to see them as the intrusion of inappropriate business ideas into the public sector, with predictable negative results. Another perspective is to regard them as a new form of government management altogether, modeled after what corporations have done (Hoggett, 1991). I am inclined to think that both observations are true: Many ideas from business have been misapplied and a new form of public management may be emerging. Bureaucratic control (centralization, formalization, specialization, and hierarchy) and professional control (collegiality, credentialism, self-regulation, semi-autonomy) seem to be giving way to postbureaucratic control (devolved control, regulated autonomy, decentralized centralism) based more on horizontal contractual relationships.

Part II of this book deals with such contractual control in pursuit of school reform. One might imagine school reform as being a contract between the reformers and school practitioners. Reformers advance their reform ideas, which practitioners judge from their own perspectives. Under what conditions are such reforms acceptable? If one conceives the problem this way, then the formidable body of knowledge about contractual relationships can be brought to bear, including the transaction cost branch of microeconomics. In the next half of the book, I develop and apply a framework for appraising reform policies, based on contractual relationships.

# PART II

# LITTLE POLICY

In the second part of this book the focus is on "little policy," what micropolicies would make a difference in the school organization itself and lead to greater productivity. So far, the argument has been that national and state education policies typically overlook critical features of schools, and hence fail. What is it about the schools that the "big policies" leave out?

One way of regarding school reforms is that the reformers are making a contract (explicitly or implicitly) with students, parents, and educational practitioners to do something different. Such contracting must cope with three critical features: the bounded rationality of organizational members, the opportunism of members, and asset specificity—that is, in this case, the investment that members have in their training, experience, and habits. Reformers typically consider teachers more altruistic, obedient, or recalcitrant than they are; overlook the knowledge required to make reforms work; and ignore the specific skills in which teachers have already invested. A framework for appraising reform policies based on these features is developed and applied to educational reforms.

These three attributes are adapted from transaction cost economics. Transaction cost economics deals with the nature of contractual relationships, how contracts are made, how they are enforced, what their costs are, what information is required by the parties involved, and what attributes of participating parties one should assume (Williamson, 1975, 1985). More generally, transaction cost economics is part of institutional economics, a relatively new branch of microeconomics concerned with how institutions develop in response to efficiency problems (Putterman, 1986). For example, one central question is whether certain functions should be obtained through markets or incorporated within the organization itself.

To begin this part of the book, there is a brief description of how schools function, including their basic technology and structure, which consists mostly of individual teachers' presenting information to passive students. One can think of different ways to improve traditional teaching and learning by changing this rather old-fashioned technology. A hypothetical "high-tech" reform of putting computers at the center of learning is presented for purposes of illustration. However, such a utopian reform could not be implemented because it ignores all three critical attributes. One would have to have quite an extensive implementation strategy for success.

Ensuing chapters appraise various proposed reforms, such as national goals, standards, and decentralization, using the same criteria. For example, national standards assume that teachers will know how to implement such standards, or that they will want to do so. Decentralization alone, on the other hand, does not provide the requisite information needed to make the schools more productive. It assumes that practitioners know how to teach more effectively if relieved of rules and regulations; most do not.

Market reforms that attempt to change the governance of the schools by opening them to market forces seriously underestimate the investment in skills and knowledge that teachers have and are determined to protect. Indeed, any workers with specific knowledge will fight to protect their investment. Market reforms, though strong on motivation, ignore the teachers' specific assets. On the other hand, market reforms pinpoint many things wrong with school bureaucracy.

Another class of reforms builds on specific assets, that is, on the teacher's knowledge and skills. Research in education often fails to be specific enough to assist teachers. Self-assessment, collecting information about a teacher's own performance, is more successful, though weak on motivation. On the other hand, small schools, organized like Central Park East, provide an excellent opportunity to develop specific knowledge about individual students and have students develop their own specific knowledge.

Finally, these themes are summarized in the conclusion of the book, with consideration of the further question of how productivity fits with other aspects of social life. After all, life is not necessarily one long sustained drive to improve productivity. The conclusion raises questions about employing an economic framework, calculative rationality based on self-interest, as the dominant basis for public policy and democracy.

# CHAPTER 6

# IMPROVING PRODUCTIVITY

As Seymour Sarason (1990) has said about attempts to reform education over the past many decades, "If anything characterizes educational reform in the past half century, it has been its ahistorical stance" (p. 34). Many things have been tried, only to fail and be tried again. Political scientist Paul Peterson (1994) is more pointed:

> Looking back over the past 25 years . . . educational governance has changed markedly. . . . People of color have gained representation; teacher organizations have become an integral part of the governing structure; states have become more involved in school finance; and federal regulations limit the authority of local school boards. But for all these changes in the politics of education, the productivity of the educational system itself seems to have changed but little. (p. xiv)

I have contended that policies intended to make education more productive fail because policymakers do not understand the schools. They don't appreciate how schools work, and they don't take critical features of the work context into account. In the next several chapters I will specify what some of these features are and employ these attributes as criteria to critique reform policies. In this chapter I briefly outline the basic structure of schools and how researchers have tried to improve their productivity, not very successfully.

## THE TYPICAL CLASSROOM

First, consider the typical classroom. Based on an extensive study of schools across the country, Goodlad (1984) characterized the basic classroom pattern this way:

- The dominant pattern of classroom organization is a group to which the teacher lectures as a whole about 70% of the time.
- Each student essentially works alone within a group setting. No student initiates much of anything.

- The teacher is the dominant figure in determining activities and the tone of the class.
- There is a paucity of praise and correction of student performance. The affective tone of the class is flat, neither positive nor negative.
- Students engage in a narrow range of classroom activities, which include listening to teachers, reading texts, answering questions, writing answers to questions, and taking tests.
- Students do not have time to finish their lessons.
- There is very little interactive technology (e.g., computers) available.
- The higher the grade level, the more the classes resemble this pattern.
- Large percentages of students report they are passively content with classroom life.
- The teachers themselves lead work lives isolated from their fellow teachers most of the time.

Certainly, this is not an inspiring learning setting in which to spend 12 or more years. Goodlad (1984) comments:

> How would I react as an adult to these ways of the classroom? I would become restless. I would groan audibly over still another seat work assignment. My mind would wander off soon after the beginning of a lecture. It would be necessary for me to put my mind in some kind of "hold" position. This is what students do. Films of relatively good frontal teaching (lecturing and questioning the total class) clearly reveal how quickly many students turn their minds elsewhere or simply doze off. (p. 233)

Of course, the organization of the school contributes substantially to this classroom pattern. "Schools are complex, busy institutions where licensed workers are responsible for batch processing the education of large groups of clients for several months at a time" (Johnson, 1990, p. 3). School organization is "cellular," with each teacher alone in his or her classroom. Teacher autonomy is necessary, uncertainty endemic (Lortie, 1975).

Furthermore, teacher pay is low, respect for teachers is lacking, and opportunities for growth and promotion are limited. For most teachers, primary rewards come from interacting with children. School buildings are poorly designed and maintained; private office space for teachers is almost nonexistent. Teachers must do their planning in crowded, noisy places. In spite of lack of privacy, they live in a world of collegial isolation.

> In the ideal world of schooling teachers would be true colleagues working together, debating about goals and purposes, coordinating lessons, observing and critiquing each other's work, sharing successes and offering solace, with the triumphs of their collective efforts far exceeding the summed accomplishments of their solitary struggles. The real world of schools is usually depicted very differently, with teachers se-

questered in classrooms, encountering peers only on entering or leaving the building. Engaged in parallel piecework, they devise curricula on their own, ignoring plans and practices of their counterparts in other classrooms or grades; when it occurs conversation offers a diversion from teaching rather than the occasion for its deliberation. (Johnson, 1990, p. 148)

The pressures of the short-term task of day-to-day teaching shoulder aside the long-term task of educating students in the truest sense. The first is an independent task, the second interdependent, requiring the cooperation of many people. Instead, norms of individualism prevail among teachers. For collegiality to flourish, as it does in universities, there must be sufficient time, supportive organizational norms, reference groups for identification and action, and administrators who encourage and accommodate—all of which are lacking (Johnson, 1990).

Of course, there is more than a passing resemblance between educational and industrial organizations (Callahan, 1962; Tyack, 1974). The American educational system was heavily influenced by Taylorism and the industrial firm of the early 20th century. The factory became the model for good management, an influence that resulted in bureaucratic central offices, rationing of instructional time, departmental structures, heavy teaching loads, blocked schedules, Carnegie units, age-graded classes, ability grouping, and an emphasis on testing and accountability.

Reformers have attempted to change this pattern, but not successfully. Most reforms try to improve education by changing teaching materials, increasing the ratio of teachers to students, grouping students differently, formulating new tests, establishing new goals, promoting higher standards, and constructing new buildings—but the basic classroom pattern remains the same, as does the organization of the school. Nor does productivity improve. In fact, productivity cannot change significantly without a major overhaul.

There is a parallel here with the revolution in auto production, which American companies have been slow to grasp. Imagine an automobile production line in which workers assemble cars in the manner introduced by Henry Ford: a moving assembly line with interchangeable parts and ease of putting them together (Womack, Jones, & Roos, 1990). The Ford method was a radical change from hand-crafted autos and resulted in much greater productivity. Although there were many adjustments to the Ford assembly methods over the years, the changes turned out to be minor compared to the basic system itself, which survived for over half a century.

Only when Toyota introduced the "lean production" system did auto manufacturing take a great leap forward in productivity. Instead of a giant die press stamping out millions of auto parts, Toyota developed a flexible die press that could be changed by the assembly workers in a few minutes, thus making possible much smaller runs. This innovation reduced the need for large inventories and permitted the detection of stamping errors, thus improving quality even while reducing costs.

Whereas Ford workers could be trained in a few minutes, and dismissed as easily, Toyota workers were given considerable responsibility and training. Lifetime employment and dedication to the company became important components. Furthermore, outside suppliers were given fixed contracts of long duration, binding them to the parent company. The system of production was so much more efficient that other manufacturers could not compete without adopting something like it.

The Toyota system has two key organizational features: It assigns the maximum number of tasks and responsibilities to the workers, adding value to the car on the line, and it has a system for detecting defects that traces every problem quickly to its cause. Unlike the Ford system, in which managers keep information to themselves, the Toyota system displays production information on an illuminated board where it can be seen from every work station. The essence is efficient teamwork.

Workers accept these challenges only when there is reciprocity, a sense that management values skilled workers, will make sacrifices to keep them, and is willing to delegate responsibilities. Often this commitment is demonstrated by symbolic actions, such as modest salaries, offices, and privileges for management (in contrast to the steep pay and privilege hierarchy of the Ford system). Simply setting up "teams" and "quality circles" doesn't work without commitment.

One might regard the educational system as incorporating a technology frozen in time and place, much like the Ford system. Reformers introduce new changes at the margin, and these may help slightly. How much difference can new teaching materials make within the basic classroom pattern? New goals? New standards? Different tests? Imagine changing the Ford production system by similar means—new production standards, new quality controls, different incentives. Surely, the increase in productivity would be marginal.

The great improvements in education have come from more schooling, adding preschool education, extending secondary education, and expanding higher education—not from changes in the classroom pattern itself. Until a significantly different system is in place, it is unlikely that there will be major improvements in productivity, whether productivity is conceived as in-depth student understanding of complex issues, more student creativity, or simply more "bang for the buck."

## A UTOPIAN REFORM

The problem is not only what to do, though that is formidable, but also how to get a new technology into place. Consider a potential reform of the basic classroom pattern. First, take the teacher out of the role of information provider, lecturing to students, which is how most classroom time is spent. Provide each student with a computer from which he or she could obtain information beautifully laid out with stunning graphics and interactive exchanges. Such an arrangement could be competitive with commercial television, the standard against which lecturers must compete (cf. Songer, 1995, 1996).

Students could proceed at their own pace with some going quickly through the material and some more deliberately. Since progress would not be impeded by the teacher plodding along at a rate the average student can absorb, there would be no need for talented or slower students to be shunted off into separate classes. Teachers could serve more as managers of learning, helping those with special problems or issues, focusing on the content of what particular students are doing, counseling, coaching, and observing individual student progress through monitors.

Computer work on core subjects might be limited to three hours in the morning when student mental acuity is greatest. In the latter part of the day teachers could arrange for group experiences—discussions, recitations, exhibitions. Joint projects and cooperative learning would be led by teachers, teacher aides, and parents acting as assistants. Each student would receive more personal attention and not suffer from lack of cooperative group work either. At the end of the day, a shortened day, students would go home (or to a fully equipped library), and teachers would have at least two hours to work with colleagues on planning and diagnosis.

Teachers could work in teams, with some specializing in technical aspects of computer work and some in group work, as well as on different subject areas. Teams could assess individual students, discussing where individuals are and where they should be directed. They could pull recorded material from student work to see exactly what the students were doing, in the same manner football coaches review videotapes of practices and games to see how individual players can improve their performance.

This is a utopian scheme for breaking out of the box of the classroom. Such an arrangement would probably improve student learning and teacher performance considerably, the way we usually measure these things. Students could proceed at their own pace and focus more on materials that interest them. Their attention would be captured by sophisticated graphics provided by commercial companies. Teachers would be released from the necessity of presenting material most of the time, though they could present when they wanted. Instead, they could concentrate on individual learning problems and group interactions. They would have time to prepare and reflect on what is happening, time that is now sorely lacking. Also, they could work with teams of other teachers, thus learning from other teachers, some of whom might be better at certain tasks. A shortened day would provide time to interact with colleagues.

However, in spite of the presumed superiority of such a "high-tech" classroom arrangement, it is not going to happen, which is the reason I have labeled it "utopian." The difficulties of getting from the classroom and schools we now have to a high-tech model are too great. First, such materials and machines are not available. They are within current technological capabilities, but few schools could afford them. Most money is tied up in day-to-day operations. When auto-mobile companies retool, they spend millions of dollars. No such sums exist for retooling schools.

But the problems of making changes are much deeper than lack of resources. Teachers don't know how to teach this way. They have learned to teach through lecturing so that is what seems necessary and sufficient to them. Most believe that students need personal lectures delivered by the teacher, not learning from a com-puter. Furthermore, what would be the advantage for them of introducing such a system? Learning to teach this way would require great effort on their part. Since most teachers receive their primary rewards through interactions with students, any scheme that takes the teacher off center stage is likely to be resisted.

Such a scheme would also require major adjustments on the part of students and parents. Some students could not adjust to the technology, as many now can-not adjust to the contained classroom. Many parents could not permit their chil-dren to come home early from school because they are at work. And, after all, teachers are supposed to be working full time, not a few hours a day, and to the public this means lecturing or grading homework. Most groups connected to schools are heavily invested in the current classroom technology, even if it is not the best imaginable.

Introducing a new teaching–learning technology is hopeless unless problems of transition to a new system can be dealt with. And these formidable problems of change cannot be solved by exhortations, appeals to altruism, or a few teacher workshops. One would need extensive resources, intensive teacher training, a huge amount of time, the cooperation of other stakeholders, and probably a different organizational form. Unfortunately, most reforms fail on these criteria.

So my criticism is not that the schools are organized like industrial produc-tion; it is that they are organized like *early 20th century* business enterprises. These early industrial organizations have been transformed or have gone out of business because they have not been able to attain sufficient flexibility and responsiveness to remain competitive. Schools have been doing what they have been doing for decades, with about the same degree of success, except that they are required to train a much larger segment of the population than before. (See Berliner & Biddle, 1995, for documentation of how schools are about as effective as they have been, which is not to say they are effective enough.)

## PRODUCTION FUNCTIONS

Research on educational productivity also supports such a pessimistic prognosis. The traditional way of examining school productivity is to look at current compo-nents of schooling through production functions. Although there is little question among economists that more years of schooling somehow result in greater learning and economic productivity (Becker, 1993), education itself has not yielded to easy analysis of how its own productivity can be improved, at least not by standard economic analyses.

Production functions take current components of schooling, such as money or teacher training or physical plant, and estimate what they contribute to educational outputs, often defined as test scores or years of schooling. For example, Hanushek (1994) has contended, "Research into the relationship between resources and student performance, conducted over the past quarter century, has demonstrated conclusively that, *within the current organization and operation of schools,* there is no consistent relationship between resources and student performance" (p. 62).

Of course, such studies do not analyze very great differences in resources among schools. There is a point at which having windows in the school, heat, and functioning toilets makes a difference, as Kozol (1991) has illustrated rather graphically. Hanushek (1994) is not talking about extreme cases such as these, however. Rather, modest increases in inputs will not make large differences in outputs. Hedges, Laine, and Greenwald (1994) have challenged Hanushek's conclusions, suggesting that resources do make discernible differences, if not radical differences:

> The pattern of results is consistent with the idea that resources matter, but allocation of resources to a specific area (such as reducing class size or improving facilities) may not be helpful in all situations. That is, local circumstances may determine which resource inputs are most effective, and local authorities utilize discretion in wisely allocating global resources among the areas most in need. (p. 11)

Nonetheless, economists and other researchers have tried more or less unsuccessfully to define a "production function" for education. In spite of 30 years of effort, an explicit set of inputs has not been consistently related to an explicit set of outputs, such as achievement test scores, with the exception of the kind of relationship defined by Hedges and his colleagues (1994). The frustration is expressed by Odden (1992): "Although educational spending, after adjusting for inflation, has increased significantly during each of the last 4 decades, student achievement has not improved or changed dramatically. . . . Policy makers would like to see higher levels of achievement for the educational investments they make" (p. 303).

Being unable to specify which inputs produce which outputs, and hence prescribe the most efficient programs, has resulted in some policymakers' turning to an "outcomes-as-standards" strategy (Monk, 1992). If one cannot define the appropriate inputs, why not specify the outputs and demand that educators produce them however they can?

> On the one hand, there is consensus that existing production function research has been largely unsuccessful at revealing the schooling outputs that dependably contrib-

ute to enhanced learning gains of students. . . . On the other hand, there is a drive toward raising the level of educational production . . . , which . . . presupposes a nontrivial store of knowledge regarding the ability of state, district, and school officials to enhance productivity. . . . The fundamental problem is that we are relying on an overly simplistic input-outcome model of educational production. (pp. 307, 314)

Monk (1992) has questioned the prospects of outcomes-as-standards policies. First, what if there is no "real" production function at all? What if there are no standard inputs related to outputs in education, as the research has suggested so far? In such a case, standards will be set and teachers will experiment but there will be no consistent results. The policy will fail. Teachers will be on their own. Teacher autonomy is the essence of practice, and the most educational authorities can do is to provide opportunities for teachers to try out different things in their classrooms in the hope that some things will work better under this circumstance.

Second, what if there is an "idiosyncratic" production function that depends on each classroom and teacher? Individual teachers might be able to discover successful strategies in their own classes during a given year, but their knowledge would not transfer to other classrooms. Hence, success would depend on individual teachers' ability to discern relationships and strategies appropriate to their particular classrooms. Over time individual teachers might be able to develop problem-solving skills that enable them to succeed more often. Teachers who are not able to discern such relationships would be less successful.

Third, if there is an explicit discoverable production function, then knowledge could be accumulated and disseminated to other schools and teachers. The outcomes-as-standards strategy, accompanied by strong central guidance, would be successful only under the last condition, and though it is too early to give up on discovering educational production functions, the evidence so far weighs against such a discovery, and against the outcomes-as-standards strategy working at this point in time.

I believe the situation that actually prevails most of the time is the second one. There are consistently successful and unsuccessful teachers. There are good teachers who are able to discover successful strategies in their own classes based on their particular students, and there are other teachers unable to do this regularly. Successful teaching is highly contextual, which means that teachers must respond to novel situations and students in each class.

What works in one class may not work in another, and what works one day may not work the next, even for the same teacher. The consistently successful teacher has strategies for discovering and monitoring what will work. But even the most successful teachers have failures sometimes. If successful teaching is so context-dependent, then attempts to discover general teaching techniques that work most of the time are doomed, at least in the current system.

Such an explanation accounts for why some teachers can be successful consistently, even though educational researchers have failed to produce consistent results about successful teaching and why economists have been unable to define educational production functions. If this analysis is correct, then strategies for improving productivity must recognize the autonomy of teachers in their classrooms and the contextual dependency of teaching success.

Analysis of the firm or organization as a production function facilitates marginal analysis within a given institutional framework but at the expense of comparative organizational features (Williamson, 1985). It tries to account for more money or training or time on task within the same institutional structure. What would such increases add at the margin? Another possibility is to radically change the system itself.

## CONCLUSION

Schools are organized to produce educational achievement in a certain fashion. Blackboards, lectures, and seat work capture the essence of the current classroom technology, with many cells of such activities constituting schools, governed by bureaucracies that have grown considerably in size over time. This is a familiar yet old-fashioned technology, with many teachers and parents believing that it is sufficient if one could only get teachers and students to execute it the right way. On the positive side, many critics underestimate the effectiveness of this technology. Historically, it has done and can do many remarkable things for a low price per student, such as assimilate immigrants, reeducate a rural population into an urban one, and achieve truly mass education.

However, if one wants significant improvements in productivity, and not only at the margin, then one must invent new technologies, as has happened in the auto industry. The old technology is limited by its very form. Although one can imagine new technologies, like high-tech classrooms with a different role for teachers, the difficulties of achieving such transformations are formidable. There are costs that come with change, and these costs for development, implementation, retraining, and information must be met in order to make the whole thing work. Reformers consistently underestimate these costs. Indeed, they often present their reforms as cost-free. However, radical transformations must be paid for by someone.

So far, attempts by educational economists and other researchers to define production functions for education, sets of inputs that lead to increased outputs, have not been successful. This is partly because of the complexity of learning, caused by its interactivity within the context in which it is embedded, and also because such analyses do not highlight the costs involved in making transformations. We turn now to a way of appraising such costs.

# CHAPTER 7

# A FRAMEWORK FOR APPRAISAL

Instead of thinking of an organization, like a school, as a production function (which doesn't seem to be a very productive activity in itself), transaction cost economics conceives organizations as structures that govern transactions among people (Williamson, 1975, 1985). Whether transactions are organized within a firm (hierarchically) or among autonomous firms (through markets) is a major consideration. Just as there are basic production costs to produce a good or service in any enterprise, there are also transaction costs, and these transactions among people and groups are highly relevant for how activities are organized. Transactions are critical in education because so much of what schools do is determined by group and individual interaction.

Transaction cost economics might be used as a rough appraisal framework to judge the possibilities of reform initiatives. I use the term "appraisal" rather than "evaluation" advisedly. Evaluation of reforms consists of collecting data after the reform is implemented. In current usage an evaluation is an empirical study of something that already exists. Appraising the plans for reform is not the same as evaluating the reforms as implemented. Appraisal also has the sense of estimating value and potential, the way a jeweler might appraise a diamond for its monetary value. In the next few chapters, I will employ transaction cost economics as a framework for appraising reform strategies.

Transaction cost economics conceives people as entering voluntary contracts (explicitly or implicitly) to do something in exchange for certain benefits. In other words transactions involve agreements among people. A particular task to be accomplished can be organized in several ways. And, one might ask, what are the comparative transaction costs involved? There are the ex ante costs of designing, negotiating, and safeguarding an agreement. And there are the ex post costs of maladaptation to the contract, haggling costs of correcting defects, set-up and running costs of governing structures, and the bonding costs of securing commitments.

The focus is on transactions among people at the micro-level, especially the comparative costs of planning, adapting, and monitoring task completion under alternative governance structures (Williamson, 1985). If one presumes that teachers and students operate on contractual "understandings" and that reformers

78

want to introduce new considerations or conditions into the educational work of the schools, improving productivity is a task that can be analyzed within this framework.

Contracting itself can be conceived as an act of planning, promise, competition, or governance, depending on what cognitive competencies and self-seeking propensities are ascribed to the agents engaged in the contractual exchange. Transaction cost economics assumes that humans are rational, but only in a limited way, so that they have "bounded rationality" (Simon, 1961). They cannot know everything or be able to process information perfectly. On the other hand, they are rational enough that many of their activities are planned with forethought.

Second, humans are opportunistic: They seek their own self-interest, sometimes aggressively. "Strong" opportunism means "self-interest seeking with guile" (Williamson, 1985, p. 47) and includes blatant forms of opportunism (cheating, lying), as well as incomplete or distorted disclosure of information in attempts to mislead, obfuscate, confuse, or disguise. In other words, not all human behavior is governed by standard ethical rules, and not all people are open and honest. This doesn't mean that all people behave opportunistically all the time but only that some people do so enough of the time that some defense against opportunism is necessary.

A weaker form of opportunism is simple lack of obedience. Presumed obedience is critical to "social engineering" schemes in which a central plan is expected to be carried out by fully obedient functionaries who identify with the overall goals, rather than following subgoals or their own self-interest. Obedience of participants is a common assumption in the utopian literature. Socialist economics, for example, typically assumes both unbounded rationality and obedience. It is assumed that people will not "take advantage" of the situation.

Third, humans often have invested specific assets of one kind or another (material assets, education, knowledge), and these vested assets can significantly affect an exchange if the investment is nontrivial. For example, financial investors must be able to seek and obtain new uses for their money when the financial arrangement they are in doesn't work out. "Redeployablity" of assets is critical. Investors are reluctant to invest money in unregulated markets unless there are safeguards, regardless of potential high returns on investment. The more safeguards and liquidity (so they can redeploy their money if necessary), the more they will invest. If such safeguards are not available, either they will not invest or they will seek significantly higher return as compensation for risk.

However, not all investments and assets are like financial resources, that is, transferable in regulated markets. Education, acquired skills, and personal contacts are often *asset specific* in that they cannot be acquired nor transferred easily. Such investments represent "sunk costs" in that the person has already paid for them with time and effort. Such "personal knowledge," in Polanyi's (1962, pp.

52–53) sense, includes skills and craftsmanship so deeply embedded in personal experience that they cannot be known by others or can be inferred only with great difficulty. Assets can be idiosyncratic:

> There exist almost unique, irreplaceable research workers, teachers, administrators: just as there exist unique, irreplaceable choice locations for plants and harbors. The problem of unique or imperfectly standardized goods . . . has been neglected in the textbooks. (Marschak, 1968, quoted in Williamson, 1985, p. 53)

Asset specificity typically arises over time. In some kinds of exchanges humans build up assets in conjunction with other particular persons, so that it is easier for them to continue to do business with those persons. In some contractual situations the specific identity of the contracting parties matters in that the relationship comes to be valued. As a result contractual and organizational safeguards arise to support these transactions over time in bilateral exchange relationships.

By contrast, in neoclassical market transactions, faceless buyers and sellers meet to exchange standardized goods at equilibrium prices. An open market is a contractual situation in which there is a uniform price available to all comers impersonally. But this does not characterize asset-specific situations. Rather, in asset-specific situations, the identity of the person with whom one is doing business does matter. Sometimes the identity of the other party is the main safeguard one has.

One example of asset-specific relationships is the contracting out of evaluation services by the National Science Foundation, discussed in detail in Chapter 4 (House, Haug, & Norris, 1996). Agency personnel develop close personal ties with contractors they know can do the work, and these contractors know how to get things done for the agency. So the relationship develops into one of bilateral dependency in a way that may not be apparent to others in the organization. The formal legal apparatus does not recognize the existence of these specific relationships.

Furthermore, not just any group can enter the contractual relationship with the same ease. Both the agency and the contractor build up assets that make it easier for them to do business with one another, assets that are not easily transferable to another partner or situation. Also, would-be rivals cannot compete at parity with the contractor on these terms, so contracting is turned into a bilateral supply arrangement over time. In such transactions personal integrity and competence come to be seen as important. One can count on certain people. It matters a great deal with whom one is doing business. These extended personal relationships may also affect the product itself.

Depending on which combination of these three attributes—bounded rationality, strong opportunism, and asset specificity—one assumes about people engaged in transactions, one can arrive at different kinds of contracting arrangements. Different combinations of these three assumed attributes are represented in Figure 7.1.

If agents are assumed to be opportunistic and have significant asset specificity

FIGURE 7.1. Attributes of the Contracting Process (adapted from Williamson, 1985, p. 31).

| Bounded Rationality | Opportunism | Asset Specificity | Implied Contracting Process |
|---|---|---|---|
| 0 | + | + | Planning |
| + | 0 | + | Promise |
| + | + | 0 | Competition |
| + | + | + | Governance |

*Note:* A "+" indicates that the attribute is sufficiently considered; a "0" indicates that it is not sufficiently considered; and a "?" indicates that there is some question as to whether the attribute is sufficiently considered.

(i.e., have invested in nontrivial specific assets), but are *un*bounded (unlimited) in their cognitive competence, the contracting process becomes "planning," where a deal is struck at the beginning of the arrangement and adhered to. Given unbounded rationality, all parties can foresee all contingent events, even those that might arise from opportunistic actions. Hence, avoidance of such events can be written into the contract by all sides. Of course, this process may assume cognitive competencies that don't exist, which is one reason why planning fails so often.

One is reminded here of "strategic planning" exercises, which have become popular in universities in recent years. Typically, university administrators, the board of governors, and a few faculty go away to a retreat for several days where they endorse a plan with university goals for all to follow. Although such planning may serve a purpose for those involved, it has little salience for faculty and students, who rarely read the strategic plan. Somehow this planning document is supposed to serve as guidance for all, but in reality it matters not (except for the symbolic value of the planning effort itself), because there is no clear conception of how the plan will be carried out.

Second, if opportunism is absent, but the other two attributes are present, then contracting becomes a matter of "promising." All agents have good intentions, pure motives, and no proclivity to serve their own self-interests excessively. Hence, both sides promise to fulfill the contracted work, which is a sufficient guarantee. If there is a problem down the line, the committed parties will resolve it with good intentions. Of course, the notion that some individuals are opportunistic some of the time is a better bet on human nature. Utopian organizations in which trust and good intentions are imputed to every member are easily exploited by those who don't share these qualities. Utopian organizations don't last long.

Conceiving organizations as production functions in which the guiding principle is "maximize firm outcomes" does not take account of such opportunistic motivations and actions. Why should participants maximize the goals of the organization, whether it be profits or test scores, especially if it costs them something? Why should they ignore what they think is important in order to pursue some overall goal? Indeed, assumptions of no opportunism mean that employees are working for the organization all the time, which seems unlikely. Safeguards against strong opportunism seem a prudent precaution.

The third situation is one in which there is no asset specificity. When no specific assets are at risk, there can be pure market competition in that the parties to the contract have no continuing interest in the identity of the other party. Hence, discrete impersonal market contracting is efficacious. An impersonal market is one in which the buyer and seller do not care who is on the other side of the transaction. They care only about price and quality of the good or service. Hence, contracting is conceived as "competition," which works when asset specificity is negligible. The absence of specific vested assets applies to a wide range of human behavior so that markets do indeed work properly in many circumstances. However, when assets are nonredeployable—the owner of the assets cannot seek a different arrangement easily—then markets do not work the same way. Those with assets at risk devise safeguards of one kind or another to protect their investments.

Transaction cost reasoning assumes that all of these contracting situations will fail often because they may be based on unrealistic assumptions. Pure planning will fail because parties have limited, "bounded" rationality and cannot see how things will work out in the future. Trying to account for all contingencies in a prespecified agreement rarely works out as planned. Simple promising breaks down because some people are opportunistic to a significant degree and will deviate from the agreement when it suits them, regardless of what was agreed to.

Pure market competition sometimes fails when people have significant specific assets at risk. Those with specific (nontransferable) assets are not inclined to put those assets at risk in unprotected market situations if they can help it. Rather they develop special relationships with their contracting partners, which provide safeguards. Hence, one should organize transactions so as to economize on bounded rationality while guarding against excessive opportunism and recognizing specific assets where they exist. This means that different governing relationships are appropriate, depending on the situation.


## APPLIED TO EDUCATION

One can apply a similar analysis to schools and school reform. The first thing is to treat students, teachers, and administrators as normal, rational people who have ambitions and motivations of their own, like everyone else. They should not be idealized to have unlikely attributes (e.g., abnormal altruism, idealism, energy, obedience). Nor should they be demonized (as unintelligent, slothful, lazy, inert). Such inaccurate characterizations serve as the unspoken basis for many misguided reforms. Teachers and students are willing and able to do certain things when they are rewarded and think these things make good sense. "Investments usually are rational responses to a calculus of expected costs and benefits" (Becker, 1993, p. 17). They are likely to resist when this is not the case. Change is not cost-free for them.

Teachers are no more prescient than anyone else, though more highly educated than the general population. They have formidable cognitive resources but cannot be expected to overcome difficult situations. "Bounded rationality" captures the situation well. On the other hand, they are not miseducated or uninformed, as some critics have implied. Teachers are also like everyone else in that some are opportunistic sometimes. They are not overwhelmingly altruistic or obedient. For example, one study found that only 11 percent of Philadelphia teachers implemented all aspects of the school district curriculum policy, only 10 percent used the proper pacing schedule, and only 4 percent complied with district grading guidelines (Johnson, 1990). Such teacher behavior is typical.

Finally, and most importantly, teachers have significant specific assets based on their education, ability, and experience in the classroom, perhaps the characteristic most misunderstood. These skills are highly specific in that they are derived from particular events, places, and students, and often consist of tacit rather than explicit knowledge, in the Polanyi (1962) sense of knowing how to do something (like ride a bicycle) without being able to explain how to do it or teach someone else to do it. These skills cannot be explicated or transferred easily. Most reformers greatly underestimate the craft knowledge that teachers possess. In fact, teachers themselves underestimate their own craft knowledge. It is not the kind of knowledge that can be recited on demand.

Given such specific attributes, one might expect teachers to be reluctant to risk their knowledge and skills in open competitive markets unless there are safeguards and expectations of significant gain. Why should teachers (or professors) work in collaborative networks of schools and universities, for example? They won't, unless they see advantages. Why should teachers risk assets built up over many years by switching to new teaching materials or techniques of doubtful quality? Their education and professional experience might be devalued.

Teachers know from experience that reformers cannot guarantee the promised outcomes of their reforms. These reforms are rarely based on careful research (not a significant source of reliable information for teachers in any case). Most reforms are the simple ideas of political and educational entrepreneurs. Almost all become fads only to disappear eventually. Why bother? And for their part, most reformers haven't the foggiest notion how their ideas will play out in schools. Distrust, and even cynicism, about new reforms is rampant among experienced teachers.

Reviewing research on the micropolitics of education, Malen (1994) says about schemes to involve teachers:

> By and large, teachers may be initially enthusiastic. But they get weary and wary. They get exhausted by the demands and become skeptical of the prospects for mean- ingful influence and suspicious of the requests for their involvement. Principals are also apprehensive. . . . These works suggest that teachers' professional security and integrity are at risk. Simply said, teachers are vulnerable to the criticisms of principals, peers, parents and students. They thus insulate themselves from the pressure and pain of interactions that can damage their reputations, diminish the quality of their work life and disrupt their ability to carry out their responsibilities in ways congruent with their views and values. (pp. 156, 157)

The situation is different for administrators. They must attend to the public and the school board. They must appear progressive (or conservative as the times demand), respond to the media, and seem to be improving the schools. That's the justification for why they hold their positions. There is small cost for them person- ally in adopting teaching innovations. For example, adopting new teaching materi- als requires administrators to get the teachers to do so. This may mean extra effort but doesn't cost administrators asset-specific resources, which for them include personal contact and knowledge of the school board. On the other hand, reforms that put their position and control at risk, such as decentralization schemes, are quite a different matter and are unlikely to be carried out as projected (Ianno- cone & Lutz, 1994).

Similar reasoning applies to students and parents. For example, students have less investment in the educational system, at least in the early years. So they are more receptive to new ideas—up to a point. However, when the rules are changed significantly, they can become extremely contentious. For instance, contemporary student riots in France have been caused by university students protesting democ- ratization of the higher education system. Such reforms threaten the specific assets they had accrued within the system. Ordinarily, it is the socialist unions of students and teachers who lead the resistance to these democratizing reforms.

Parents also have investments in moving their children along in the educa- tional system to achieve social mobility for them. Since World War II, social mo- bility has been achieved primarily by people entering the professions, for which higher education is the gatekeeper. For example, a reform like doing away with grades (the giving of marks) in the elementary schools seems a simple reform that most would applaud. Students should be overjoyed to be relieved of grading pres- sures, and teachers would not have to deal with an odious task. However, grades are an important control mechanism for some teachers, and there is an under- standing in many classrooms that if students behave and do minimal work, they will receive a passing grade. Furthermore, most middle-class parents are adamant about maintaining grades. It provides them with a way of knowing whether their children are on the right track and gives their children a differential advantage in the competition for entry to higher education. Eliminating grades usually results in a strong backlash from parent groups.

Although it sometimes appears that the schools don't change because of a paucity of ideas and energy, that they are inert, their lack of innovativeness is more often caused by vested interests pulling in different directions. The schools are the way they are partly for historical reasons and partly because they are the result of constant pressures from different directions. The groups doing the tugging— teachers, students, parents, and taxpayers—share attributes of bounded rationality, opportunism, and asset specificity. Policies to change the schools must take these things into consideration at risk of failure.

## THE TEACHERS' SPECIFIC ASSETS

One of the things most difficult for outsiders to understand about teachers is that teachers have special knowledge and skills that enable them to conduct their business. Outsiders believe that teachers simply need knowledge of a content area, say mathematics, to lecture to students. But teaching is far more complex than this and is based on specific knowledge and skills acquired over a period of time. Of course, some teachers are not very good at it, while others are superb. How are these skills acquired?

Imagine a situation in which a person is learning to teach for the first time, say an instructor is faced with teaching her first class, an introductory educational psychology course to undergraduates. How does she proceed? Does she review the research literature in search of causal regularities between teaching and learning such as, for example, the relationship between positive reinforcement and learning curves? After all, this is the content she will be teaching to these future teachers.

Such a prospect seems highly unlikely. A far more probable scenario is that over the years she has had teachers that she thought were particularly effective or ineffective. She tries to remember what they did that worked with classes in which she was a student, as well as what didn't work very well. Based on her own experiences in the classroom as a student, she has notions of cause-and-effect relationships, of what works and doesn't work. Some of these ideas may well be mistaken but she holds them nonetheless.

From this repertoire of ideas and techniques, she selects notions around which to organize her classes initially. Some cause-and-effect relationships that she thinks effective she either cannot do or they do not fit her overall style. For example, she decides that small-group work, although effective when used by some teachers at some times, doesn't really fit with her own experiences as a student, in which small groups seemed hazy and unfocused. She decides to direct the class discussion herself, using the class as a whole. In addition, she remembers that she never liked teachers who assigned work but graded it tardily. She vows to return the students' graded papers the following class period. The students will accept reasonably rigorous grading, she reasons, if they perceive it as quick and fair.

How many of these considerations will there be? Ten? Fifty? No doubt it depends on the person and the situation. There will be many. What they have in common is that most will be based on the new teacher's actual experience as a student *participating* in former classes. A student, after all, is a participant rather than merely an observer. But even all this is only preparatory to learning to teach—trying out these ideas in the classroom. One can be a passenger on a car trip and learn something about where one has been, but when one is the driver of the car the learning is more intense and permanent. Many of us can drive to a location only one time and can retrace our route exactly years later. The new teacher is now the driver of the classroom and what she has learned tentatively will be validated or invalidated in the course of her actions in the classroom.

As the new teacher begins to teach, the general considerations of how to act (Should she be highly organized? Authoritative? Flexible? Well-dressed?) give way to more specific considerations of exactly what to do (Should she lecture? Lead group discussions? Show movies?). The easiest thing for her to do is to lecture, to tell facts and stories, and she does this first. She is certain of her ability to control the class through her knowledge and less certain of her ability to interact with students or lead a discussion. So she lectures initially.

As her confidence grows she adds to her teaching repertoire. Although as a student she has never liked small groups, she finds that if she makes the group task small enough and specific enough, the students can stay focused. She discovers that the students really love the small groups but still her previous small-group experience was not positive, and she does not fully trust small-group work in spite of her students' reaction.

As she gradually tries out new things, she sometimes encounters difficult problems. For example, she cannot seem to teach moral development properly. In her first classes she presents Kohlberg's (1969) and Gilligan's (1982) theories of moral development but somehow the ideas "bounce off" the students. The lessons don't "work," and by not working she means that the students cannot discuss the ideas in class, cannot talk about the subject, and have no conception of morality even though they can answer the short items on her tests. Perhaps they do not have enough background.

The next semester she assigns extra readings on the topic. The lessons still do not work. She talks to colleagues, wondering what to try next. In her third semester she attempts a different approach. She begins the topic by presenting the students with a moral problem, in which a black woman is rejected by a sorority because of her race. She has the students discuss these two situations in small groups, answering questions she has prepared for them, then discusses the situations with the whole group.

For the next class she has the students read Kohlberg's theory of moral development to see how the students' specific discussions fit Kohlberg's hierarchy of moral levels. The students are appalled to find themselves operating at the lower levels of moral development. They are upset, ask questions, become engaged. In the third and final class she has the students fit the examples to Gilligan's theory of moral development in women. Now the students have ideas and a vocabulary, and, most importantly, can talk about the topic. As further proof of success, some students choose moral development as a topic for their term papers, which none had ever done before. Even though the students do no better on her tests than before, the teacher is now satisfied that the lessons work.

Although the new teacher experiments, she changes only one thing at a time. She will try a new textbook, but nothing else new. She will change the assignments but nothing else. Often she has no idea of how a change will work in practice— she must always assess its success in the classroom. By trying out only one new thing at a time, she not only simplifies her assessment but also remains in control, assured that her class will still be a good one in spite of her experimentation.

The new teacher is learning cause-and-effect relationships through direct participation, through participating first as a student and then as the teacher. This direct experience is gained mostly by performing and acting rather than by passively observing, and this direct personal experience is so intense and powerful that it shapes what the teacher will do and try to do throughout her career. After a few years her learning rate will decline because she will feel she has mastered her environment. Her teaching repertoire will be largely formed.

One may well wonder if this is the proper way for the teacher to proceed. Perhaps this is an ineffective teacher who has learned the wrong things. In fact, this is an actual case and during her first semester, this teacher was placed on the university list of excellent teachers, which was determined by comparing her scores on a student response instrument with those of other instructors in the university. By her second semester her scores were among the top 10% of excellent teachers.

The teacher has something in mind, tries it out, and judges its success or failure. The determination of whether the lesson works is based largely on firsthand experience, on performing, and through those experiences the teacher develops a personal set of cause-and-effect inferences about teaching. They may well be mistaken but mostly they are not. The teacher can develop a reasonable set of inferences to guide her through the day, just as most of us manage to drive our cars to work, feed ourselves, and conduct our daily affairs. All this is not ordinarily a problem, except perhaps when the car won't start, which is not to say that either our lives or the teacher's performance cannot be improved. It is to say that most of what we do is rational and makes good sense.

In summary, teachers learn to teach primarily through direct experience and participation, first as students, then as beginning teachers. From direct experience teachers draw cause-and-effect inferences as to what works and doesn't work for them. This knowledge is personal and particular to the actual situation, and much of it is tacit: The teacher knows how to do things he or she cannot explain. This knowledge has primacy when it comes to actually teaching classes and shapes much of what teachers do throughout their careers. This is asset-specific knowledge. Any strategy for improving education must work through this basic fact. (This section was based on House & Lapan, 1988; House, Lapan, & Mathison, 1989; and House, Mathison, & McTaggert, 1989, all influenced strongly by Schön, 1983.)

## CONCLUSION

One might conceive of reforming schools as a contract between the reformers and those who must undertake the reforms, namely, the teachers, students, administrators, and parents. Transaction cost economics provides an analysis of such a contracting relationship based on the attributes one ascribes to the parties to the contract. The three critical attributes are bounded rationality (people have limited cognitive abilities), opportunism (people work for their own self-interest), and specific assets (people accrue valuable assets they cannot transfer elsewhere easily). These three attributes result in dynamics that must be considered if the contractual relationship is to be successful.

These attributes apply to education. Teachers and students are bounded in their rationality, opportunistic some of the time, and accrue certain assets in the system. They are not particularly altruistic, rationalistic, or recalcitrant. Rather, they undertake activities in which they can see benefits. They are willing to make investments as rational responses to expected costs and benefits. Most reforms are not well thought through by reformers, and this is apparent to those in the system. Those in the system have an investment in it, even if they know it is not the best of all possible worlds. However, to get them to change requires more than rhetoric.

Perhaps the least understood feature as it applies to teachers is their specific assets. For the most part, teachers learn to teach in the classroom on their own. This takes many years and is not an easy process. The knowledge of how to teach is mostly tacit. It cannot be recited on demand. And much of this knowledge is context-specific: what to do with these students in this place with this subject matter. When this knowledge of how to do things in the classroom is threatened, teachers will try to protect their investment, as any rational investor would, even if it is a cognitive investment.

# CHAPTER 8

# GOALS, STANDARDS, AND DECENTRALIZATION

Consider how some educational reforms might stack up against criteria from the transaction cost framework. Most reforms ignore critical attributes. As I have indicated with the utopian reform example of a high-tech classroom, teachers do not have the knowledge to manage such classes (bounded rationality), they have specific assets invested in the current teaching role (strong asset specificity), and some would take advantage by doing little teaching at all unless safeguards were employed (opportunism). Some would call students away from the computers and lecture to them. Similar analyses could be conducted for how students and parents would adjust.

Figure 8.1 indicates whether the three main factors are considered sufficiently in various reform proposals.

## NATIONAL GOALS

One prominent plan for educational reform is *America 2000,* begun in the Bush administration and continued by the Clinton administration as Goals 2000 (U.S. Department of Education, 1991). This plan combines the establishment of national goals with national standards, albeit voluntary ones. However, there are other goal programs without such standards, so that one can advocate goals without explicit standards. The basic idea of national goals is that schools are unfocused. There are too many goals, too many interest groups, and too many purposes for the school to serve. The result is lack of direction.

Hence, if one can focus on fewer goals, the productivity of schools will improve significantly. The critical question is why teachers and others would pursue the national goals rather than state, local, or personal goals. Announcing a set of goals does nothing to establish those goals in schools and classrooms, unless one

FIGURE 8.1. Attributes of Educational Reforms I.

| Bounded Rationality | Opportunism | Asset Specificity | Reforms |
|---|---|---|---|
| 0 | 0 | 0 | Utopian "high-tech" |
| 0 | 0 | + | National goals |
| ? | 0 | + | National standards |
| 0 | + | + | Standards–New York |
| + | 0 | + | Educator networks |
| 0 | 0 | + | Decentralization |
| 0 | ? | + | U-form hierarchy |
| + | + | + | M-form hierarchy |

Note: A "+" indicates that the attribute is sufficiently considered; a "0" indicates it is not sufficiently considered, and a "?" indicates that there is a question as to whether the attribute is sufficiently considered.

assumes that teachers are especially altruistic or obedient. So motivation is lacking, if one assumes that teachers are like everyone else. Would professors pursue national goals for universities? Physicians for medicine? Businessmen for business? It seems unlikely. In fact, Goodlad (1984) found that teachers and parents think schools should be comprehensive, which means caring for student well-being across the board, a view that would work against narrow goals.

Furthermore, if goals were defined more precisely, would teachers be able to achieve them? Drug-free schools? First in the world in math and science education by the year 2000? Every child coming to school ready to learn? The attainment of these goals demands resources and knowledge far beyond the reach of ordinary teachers and administrators. They wouldn't know how to accomplish these goals, even if they wanted to. Perhaps that is why the national goals are joked about so often among professional educators. (One joke is that "First in math and science in the world by the year 2000" was a typographical error meant to be "First in the world in 2,000 years.")

Goal specification does acknowledge that teachers have asset-specific abilities and skills. New goals do not require teachers to abandon their own skills and abilities developed over time. So this is a good characteristic. But the plan is deficient in not recognizing opportunism and bounded rationality. Its chances of improving educational productivity would seem to be slight.

## STANDARDS

Another reform is to have goals and standards combined in content-standard schemes. The national standards might be subject-matter standards developed by professional organizations, such as the National Council of Teachers of Mathematics, the good example cited by almost everyone. The presumption is that teachers don't have the proper focus, or the correct content either. Content standards specify in some detail what students should be expected to know. And teachers can achieve this knowledge however they deem fit.

This approach assumes that the motivation for teachers to adopt such standards will be provided by publicity given to test scores based on the standards and to the prestige accorded material developed by professional organizations. Such an approach overestimates the degree to which teachers will adopt standards and miscalculates how teachers will react if their students' test scores are made public. The history of such attempts is rampant with teachers' teaching the test items under conditions of strong accountability and manipulating or distorting the scores (opportunism). This approach also misjudges teachers' ability to achieve the recommended outcomes. There is some attention to motivation, but it is insufficient. And there is attention to providing what to teach (through the standards) but it is insufficient too, at least as it now stands. (In the accompanying figures I have inserted a "+" when the attribute is sufficiently considered, a "0" when it is not sufficiently considered, or a "?" when there is more than one version of a reform that may differ on this attribute or else I do not have enough information to make the judgment of whether the attribute is sufficienty considered. One needs more specific information to make the judgment.)

There are other types of standards reforms. In the 1980s many states and localities passed rules and regulations designed to make education more difficult, for example, more required years of particular subject areas, higher grade point averages for graduation or admission, and so forth. The general belief now is that these requirements did not produce significant reform. An example discussed before was New York City's Promotional Gates Program. Promotional Gates took motivation seriously, but overestimated the cognitive resources of the teachers. It assumed that teachers and students were not working hard enough and sought to induce them to work harder by establishing an automatic failing mechanism (opportunism).

However, it also assumed that teachers would know what to do to help students pass the tests or else could learn what to do in a summer workshop. As it turns out, educational research indicates that flunking students will significantly increase their chances of dropping out of school altogether (Shepard & Smith, 1989). In fact a year or two after the reform, students were not succeeding any better than before. Most reforms are not well informed about relevant research. On the other hand, this approach did respect the assets of the teachers.

## EDUCATOR NETWORKS

Several educators have established "networks" of schools, universities, businesses, and community groups. These include Jesse Jackson's PUSH/Excel, John Goodlad's "Partnership for Schools," Ted Sizer's "Coalition of Essential Schools," and Henry Levin's "Accelerated Schools." As worthwhile as these endeavors might be, the originators themselves probably would not contend that these networks by themselves are sufficient for significant reform. Most networks try to incorporate other activities (discussed later). The networks take cognizance of the teachers' assets and try to improve on them, and they try to expand the teacher's bounded rationality. However, sometimes they do not provide sufficient motivation or follow-through. Professors are paid to teach classes and do research, not to work with public schools. While many good things might result from such networks, teachers and professors are not sufficiently motivated.

On the other hand, some networks have sprung from the conceptions of charismatic leaders who inspire and motivate but whose efforts disintegrate when the leader leaves or the operation is transformed from a charismatic movement to a bureaucratized operation. Followers either cannot or will not maintain the original inspiration. This was true for Jesse Jackson's PUSH/Excel network, which was highly inspirational but fell apart in most places for lack of ideas of what to do next (bounded rationality) and because people transformed the program to their own purposes (opportunism). Jackson's program also ran into strong racial politics (House, 1988).

Muncey and McQuillan (1993a, 1993b) found something similar in their study of the Coalition of Essential Schools, though without the racial element. They found that there was not a consensus in the schools that fundamental changes needed to occur; that significant differences existed among faculty as to what to do; that some faculty (often women and new faculty) became involved but their efforts divided the rest of the faculty politically; and that Coalition teachers were unprepared to deal with conflict. The Coalition took the form of a social moment but was unable to endure in many places after bureaucratization. The introduction of change efforts frequently led to Coalition teachers' being perceived as receiving favored treatment and resources, which created dissension among the rest of the faculty. Of course, these same problems occur in the introduction of other reforms.

## DECENTRALIZATION

In analyzing the movement to push decisions to the school or classroom level, Ferris (1992) noted, "A key premise of the decentralization movement in education policy is that those at the school site have information necessary for the decisions to enhance educational performance, information that is not available at the district level or above" (p. 333). The comparative advantage of decentralization is based on the idea that those closest to students are in the best position to judge their needs. However, just because the requisite information is not available at the district or higher levels doesn't mean it is available at the school or classroom level. It is one thing to be freed from bureaucratic strictures. It is quite another to know what to do with this freedom.

Authentic decentralization takes full advantage of the asset specificity of the teacher's skills and knowledge. (One must speak of "authentic" decentralization because many decentralization plans do not really devolve authority to lower levels.) On the other hand, one must be concerned about whether teachers and administrators know how to improve things and also about opportunism, whether they will do the appropriate things rather than pursue subgoals.

Ferris (1992) has applied "principal-agent" theory to decentralization efforts. Principal-agent theory treats decentralization as a contract between the granting authority, the "principal" (the school district or state), and the "agent" (the school or teacher). The principal must worry about whether the agent is performing properly. The cost of enforcing such a contract depends on the measurability of the agent's behavior (e.g., effort) and performance (outcome). The more uncertain the relationship between behavior and outcome, the more the principal must invest in gathering information. The more expensive the cost of collecting information, the more the contract is likely to be based on behavior rather than outcome.

One problem with measuring performance is the lack of adequate performance measures. Standardized tests are the usual way of measuring school outcomes but there are long-standing problems with tests as accurate measures of outcome. There have been efforts to develop "alternative assessment" measures, but good alternative tests do not currently exist, as discussed earlier, and alternative testing can be very expensive. Few teachers would be willing to have their teaching judged on the basis of student test scores. In fact, a recurrent problem is that teachers under pressure teach students the test items (opportunism).

There are two problems with applying principal-agent theory to schools: Competitiveness among agents is not a factor, and schools do not have a single principal to report to. Rather, schools serve many constituencies. Ferris (1992) concludes that a change in locus of decision making may be necessary but is not sufficient for improving schools. Either one must find teachers who know how to make things happen or one must retrain teachers somehow. Decentralization is promising but its success depends on what is done after the decentralization.

This analysis seems to be borne out by events in the Chicago schools, the most renowned decentralization plan. Each school is run by a local council composed of parents, teachers, and elected officials. However, once these councils take over, often nothing different happens in classrooms. One study concluded, "These cases strongly suggest that no amount of increased commitment and no amount of increased competence will substantially alter the educational lives and achievement of children" (North Central Regional Educational Laboratory, 1992, p. 165). After 3 years only changes at the margins had occurred. Also, the Chicago reform has been played out against a backdrop of strong racial tensions. Significant changes in the governance of the schools do not necessarily lead to changes in the classroom. It is still early for the Chicago reform, although the mayor's office had attempted to reassert central authority as this book went to press, not a good omen for the reform.

In summary, decentralization is important, perhaps even necessary for school reform, but not sufficient. Some ways must be found to cope with the bounded rationality of teachers, administrators, and board members, and the potential opportunism threatened by such a shift.

## GOVERNANCE AND HIERARCHY IN SCHOOLS

Both decentralization and market reforms target the administrative hierarchy as a key obstacle to school reform. Certainly, the bureaucratic structure is too top heavy for change to occur. In *The Politics of Educational Innovation* (1974), I suggested there were two pathways to achieve more innovation. One would be to increase hierarchical control to force more innovation, the way that has been tried over the past 20 years without much success. More regulations, requirements, and mandates have not resulted in improved quality. The other way, the recommended one, was to increase collegial authority, which has yet to be tried to a significant degree, though I will discuss this later. A third way, the market mechanism, has now become popular as an idea.

Administrative hierarchy has become a problem rather than a solution. Administrative structures absorb a huge share of the school budget. For example, in the New York City schools, only 43% of the budget is spent in classrooms, a figure in line with other large city schools, according to the Council of Great City Schools (Steinberg, 1996). In 1995, of the $6,284 spent per student in regular classrooms in New York City, $2,554 per student went for teachers' salaries, $64 for teachers' aides, and $40 for textbooks. Costs per student *external* to the classroom included city administration ($746), district administration ($159), the principal's office ($485), as well as building services, such as custodial ($580), and support services, such as the cafeteria and transportation ($500). The mind boggles at the cost of the infrastructure. No wonder spending more money for schools is a hard sell.

Not only does the administration absorb huge amounts of resources; whenever anyone wants to initiate a new program either from the inside or outside, one must navigate through dense mazes of administrators. In large city schools on average, the hierarchy has grown from 1 administrator per 18 teachers in 1956 to 1 in 12 in 1978, a 30% increase (Wong, 1995). In large districts there might be eight layers of administrators between the superintendent and the teachers. The start-up costs of attempting something new are huge even if one is sucessful. Furthermore, in the meantime administrators are issuing edicts and regulations with which teachers must contend, even if only to evade them and even if the edicts will be reversed next day or next week. Schools cannot be productive unless they are relieved of this immense administrative burden that they carry in addition to trying to teach children.

So, as advocates of decentralization have rightly contended, the administrative hierarchy must be reduced. However, the solution is not to throw out the administrative structure altogether. No restructured corporations have done so, even though many have decentralized operations and reduced administrative staffs. In reviewing corporate hierarchies, Williamson (1985) says:

> Rarely, I submit, will optimum job design involve the elimination of hierarchy. Instead, it entails taking the rough edges off of hierarchy and affording those workers who desire it a greater degree of interested involvement. But it is no accident that hierarchy is ubiquitous within all organizations of any size. (p. 270)

Many corporations have been transformed from centralized, departmentalized, unitary administrative structures (called the U-form of corporate governance), or from holding company structures that try to manage autonomous divisions (the H-form), into multidivisional corporate structures (the M-form). Central staffs of centralized, unitary structures simply could not keep up with information and the key decisions that had to be made at the divisional level.

By attending to overwhelming administrative detail, corporations using this structure had no ability to pursue entrepreneurial activities. These companies ceased to be innovative and responsive to their environments. Short-run operational tasks overwhelmed long-run strategic considerations. Of course, this is the type of corporate structure on which the American school system is modeled— the unitary, centralized structure that has become all but ineffective and nonresponsive (Callahan, 1962; Tyack, 1974).

On the other hand, in a holding company, like General Motors at one time, the central office lost control altogether. Separate divisions went their own way, doing what was best for the division but not necessarily for the company. Divisions overinvested in their own operations because they were reluctant to return savings to other divisions or the central office. Central policy was determined by bargaining among division managers, so that internal political trade-offs provided erratic direction for the company. (This characterizes autonomous departments bargaining among themselves in universities.)

The eventual corporate solution was the multidivisional form of structure in which operations were removed from planning, monitoring, and allocation. Daily operations are managed by semi-autonomous divisions, which are profit centers unto themselves. They have the autonomy to make decisions that affect operations because it is assumed that only they have the appropriate information at the local or divisional level to make good decisions. The central office concentrates on long-range planning and entrepreneurial activities. It

- identifies separate activities within the firm
- maintains a quasi-autonomous standing to each
- monitors the efficiency performance of each
- awards incentives
- allocates cash flows
- and performs strategic planning.

In a sense, this structure takes advantage of both central and decentralized information processing. Operational decisions can be made at the local level where people are more likely to have the requisite knowledge, and strategic decisions can be made at the central level for overall direction of the firm. This structure addresses the potential opportunism of the decentralized structure by allowing the center to monitor and reallocate resources to best advantage.

Given the "bottom-heavy" technology of schooling, where decisions are necessarily made at the classroom and building level, the M-form hierarchy makes sense for school districts, rather than the U-form organization that school districts have now, or the H-form, which they would be likely to have if every school became autonomous. If each school were autonomous, one might see bargaining among them such as exists among university departments. The M-form takes advantage of a decentralized technology, in which teachers exhibit much asset specificity and establish bilateral relationships with students, while at the same time providing guidance, direction, and reallocation where needed.

For example, one can imagine such a district structure increasing the variety of schooling through charter school possibilities, deliberately creating new schools that are different, thus improving the supply side of schooling. Of course, new schools would need more resources in their start-up phase, and the M-form district could provide such allocations, as well as monitor schools for performance to make sure they did not violate norms of racial integration, and so forth. In most districts schools follow the same rules, which makes variety difficult to achieve.

The central office must also evaluate and monitor school performance, but this requires more than collecting test scores. Evaluation requires a specific context in which to make judgments about how the school is functioning. There is no such thing as context-free evaluation because any number of factors must be considered to arrive at overall judgments about performance. Evaluation is context-specific. Hence, the central office must be far enough away to permit autonomy, yet close enough to allow evaluation of performance. State and national offices are too far removed for such a function.

Bureaucratic control consists of centralization, formalization, and specialization, while professional control consists of self-regulation, collegiality, credentialism, and semi-autonomy (Hoggett, 1991). By contrast, postbureaucratic control consists of devolved control, decentralization, formalized informalism, and regulated autonomy. Autonomy is allowed *within boundaries*. Organizations are able to be more innovative but still have sense of direction.

> Post-bureaucratic organisational regimes recognise the inevitability of human agency within organisational life and therefore seek to formalise freedoms for it. Managerial devolution is therefore equivalent to "freedom within boundaries." (Hoggett, 1991, p. 251)

As in liberal democracies, people exercise freedoms within agreed-on frameworks of conduct. Also as in democracies, the organizations must rely heavily on socialization processes to regulate behavior. The center must support the organizational culture and mission, establish expected results, and monitor performance.

## CONCLUSION

Different proposed educational reforms can be appraised using the transaction cost criteria to see if the three critical attributes are considered sufficiently. National goals lack sufficient consideration of opportunism and bounded rationality. Why should teachers pursue distant goals, and would they know how to accomplish such ambitious goals if they did? National standards ignore opportunism and maybe bounded rationality as well. Most attempts to closely monitor teachers by using tests for accountability purposes have resulted in distorted information. Whether standards strategies ignore bounded rationality depends on the information provided teachers. On the other hand, these two reforms do acknowledge the specific assets of teachers.

Decentralization reforms in general ignore bounded rationality and opportunism as well. Just because a district administrative structure is decentralized doesn't mean that suddenly teachers and administrators will know what to do for more effective education. Nor does it mean they will pursue the goals they are supposed to, rather than their own subgoals. Decentralization is a step, most probably a necessary step, toward effective school reform, but not a sufficient one in itself.

One must acknowledge that the huge and cumbersome administrative structures of school districts are serious impediments to change. Similar problems have plagued American corporations. The solution, however, is not to do away with administrative hierarchy altogether. Rather, the best solution is to develop a multidivisional form of organizational structure so that a small central staff removed from day-to-day operations plans the overall strategy of the organization, allocates money, and monitors performance, leaving operational decisions at the local level. This allows the school level opportunities to change and the central administration opportunity to start new enterprises.

# CHAPTER 9

# MARKET AND INCENTIVE POLICIES

Given the strong influence of economic rationales underlying most reform efforts, it is not surprising that some of the most powerful concepts and ideas for reform have been taken directly from business and economics. The economist Hanushek (1994) is straightforward in his view about the proper direction for school reform:

> Economic issues motivate the movement to reform America's schools. Despite ever rising school budgets, student performance has stagnated. Disappointing student performance, in turn, contributes to disappointing economic growth, stagnating living standards, and widening gaps among the incomes of different social and ethnic groups. Yet, although economic issues are central to the problems of education, economic ideas have been notably, and most unfortunately, absent from plans for reform. (p. xv)

Two ideas given great currency in the media, government, and academia are market and incentive policies applied to schools, including school vouchers, schools of choice, merit pay, performance incentives, "contracting out" services, and business-operated schools. There is also considerable discussion about how schooling serves (or fails to serve) business enterprises and employment opportunities, with some reformers recommending that businesses themselves take on educational functions (Hollenbeck, 1993). In this chapter I will discuss market policies, as manifested in schools of choice, and incentive policies applied to teachers.

## MARKET POLICIES

The most influential work to propose that the public schools abandon control through elected school boards and resort to market mechanisms in which parents have freedom to send their children to whatever schools they want at public expense is Chubb and Moe's *Politics, Markets, and America's Schools* (1990; Chubb, 1988). These two political scientists contend that parental choice would free schools from bureaucratic control and that student achievement would improve because schools would be more autonomous, and hence able to increase achievement.

In their opinion the "laundry list" of school reforms (additional standards and regulations) initiated in the 1980s had no chance of succeeding. The basic impediment to reform is democratic control of schools. Even though we know what makes for a good school (from the "effective schools" literature), we are not able to incorporate such features into schools. School goals are countless in number, lack coherence, and are watered down to please numerous constituencies.

Democratic control results in bureaucratic mandates and edicts being imposed from above, leaving little room for teachers and administrators to do what they know best. In Chubb and Moe's view, "What [schools] are supposed to do depends on who controls them and what those controllers want them to do" (1990, p. 30). The winners of political contests impose their values on schools. That's how democratic politics works, and this imposition of values weakens the schools' overall effectiveness because it takes decision making away from workers at the site level. Education is a process that requires that critical decisions be made on the spot, in the school and classroom.

In imposing policies, policymakers assume incorrectly that officials and teachers will harness their energies toward these policies. Multiple interest groups make compliance with external policies less likely because attention must be paid to those constituencies. Faced with this situation, the best solution for those who govern is to bureaucratize what is wanted through mandates. Mandates make changing course difficult in case those in power lose power. So political factions try to impose their will on schools by mandates and bureaucracy.

However, in Chubb and Moe's (1990) analysis, schools cannot be controlled effectively from above because measuring output properly is so problematic as to be impossible. "The only way to measure performance adequately is to rely on the discretion of those who work in the school—which is precisely what the unions and democratic authorities are strongly inclined not to do, and what the whole system is built to prevent" (p. 197). The technology of schooling is local ("bottom-heavy") in that people in the school must decide what to do if effective education is to occur.

> To put it most generally: schools and their personnel are granted a measure of discretion by technical necessity, but detailed formal specifications in legislative mandates and administrative regulations are voluminously imposed on all concerned, so that the schools' scope for discretionary action is sharply narrowed—and the discretion that remains is then insulated from political control through extensive reliance on civil service, tenure, (nominal) professionalism, and other structural means. (Chubb & Moe, 1990, p. 45)

By contrast, if there were a market system for school choice, school personnel would be able to exercise their knowledge more effectively, and schools would have to produce what parents want. In a market arrangement, parents would have their interests more forcefully represented. In fact, their preferences would be more important than those of other groups. Those who operate the schools would have to please the "clients" (parents and students) because parents could switch their children to other schools. Schools that did not perform satisfactorily would go out of business from loss of clients. In such a system bureaucratic strictures would lessen because the overgrown apparatus of administrative control would not be needed. Homogenous goals and constituencies for each school would produce less bureaucracy.

Chubb and Moe (1990) present an elaborate plan for school choice. The state would set minimal criteria for schools, as is done for private schools now. All applicants meeting the state's minimal goals would receive public money. Schools would be reimbursed on a per capita student basis by a state "choice office." Transportation to school would be provided to students and there would be a state information center dispensing information about schools. The results would be a transformation of the schools. "Choice is a panacea. . . . It has the capacity all by itself to bring about the kind of transformation that, for years, reformers have been seeking" (Chubb & Moe, 1990, p. 216).

The authors back up their claims empirically. Using data from Coleman, Hoffer, and Kilgore's (1982) public versus private schools study, Chubb and Moe (1990) create a variable of "school autonomy" and relate it to student achievement. In their analysis, student achievement is higher in schools that are more autonomous. However, Glass and Matthews (1991) have severely criticized their empirical claims. Taking Chubb and Moe's empirical analysis at face value, their statistical model accounts for only 5% of the variance in student achievement. A school that moved from the 5th percentile on autonomy to the 95th percentile would increase its student achievement by only one month grade equivalent, a minuscule amount. Furthermore, there are a number of things wrong with the data analysis itself. Glass and Matthews conclude, "It [the book] is rather a polemic wrapped in numbers" (p. 26).

Howe (1997) is also critical of the analysis. In his critique, a consumer choice scheme should focus on the satisfaction of client preferences as the ultimate criterion, not student achievement. If client satisfaction is most important, then achievement is conditional. Some parents might put it first; some might not. In fact, there is evidence that parents do not choose student achievement as the primary goal of schools (Goodlad, 1984). Rather, parents want schools to accomplish a wide range of academic, personal, social, cultural, and vocational goals—just what Chubb and Moe (1990) are trying to avoid. In giving student achievement such an important place, Chubb and Moe have imposed their own "higher values" on the schools, which they disdain in others.

Second, there is no evidence that parental choice (or even school autonomy) does increase student achievement. Parents tend to choose schools based on many factors, including convenience and racism, criteria that have little to do with achievement (Howe, 1997). Finally, Chubb and Moe (1990) assume that society will be better off with schools catering to parental preferences without considering the social problems that might arise from such privatization. In other words, there may be social effects unaccounted for, such as increased inequality and segregation.

Chubb and Moe's (1990) data analysis appears to be badly flawed. They have made too many errors to provide credible empirical support for their thesis. However, statistical analysis aside, what about their main argument that the schools would be better off by responding to market forces? They have a valid point that the schools are heavily bureaucratic, that these restrictions severely impede teaching and learning, and that variety (truly different types of schools) is lacking. From a market perspective schools are deficient on the supply side as well as the demand side. Perhaps Chubb and Moe's most compelling insight is to treat schools as institutions. They make a plea that schools should be regarded as total institutions rather than looking simply at what happens inside them.

However, I do not think they have gone far enough in their conceptual analysis. Schools are indeed impeded by their bureaucracy and by having to serve many different constituencies. But does the heavy bureaucracy stem primarily from democratic control? Business corporations also have developed large, inefficient bureaucratic organizations, and they are certainly not democratically controlled. In fact, there is considerable evidence from the history of education that school administrators organized schools to emulate businesses, as demonstrated in Callahan's (1962) classic study, *Education and the Cult of Efficiency*. The bureaucratic organization and sameness of the schools doesn't seem to derive from democratic control in any direct way. However, it is true that trying to respond to many diverse constituencies does make educational change difficult, since people want to go in quite different directions.

Responding to many constituencies often produces no change because many constituencies can effectively veto it (Iannaccone & Lutz, 1994). It is also true that responding to constituencies increases the administrative bureaucracy by adding services to deal with these constituencies. Higher education is a dramatic example in which administrative costs soared by 60% in the 1980s, compared with a 6% increase in faculty costs (Massy & Wilger, 1992). However, these bureaucratic escalations have occurred in both private and public institutions.

Certainly, the bureaucracy needs to be reduced. But new ways of organizing the work are needed also. Chubb and Moe (1990) are correct in arguing that school technology is bottom-heavy in that school personnel on the spot must make critical decisions that cannot be dictated effectively from above. Furthermore, the nature of the educational process is so complex as to defy quality measurement that can provide a simple reading for those in power, a fact Chubb and Moe recognize but that most policymakers do not. One might think of organizing the work in decentralized teams and supplying information to those teams.

Chubb and Moe (1990) assume that teachers and administrators know what to do if only they were not restrained by bureaucratic impediments. Eliminate the bureaucracy and all will be well. But this is not the case. Most decentralized schools operate much like other schools, and experience with decentralization reforms indicates that teachers and administrators don't do things differently once the rules and regulations are removed, though such freeing up may be a necessary condition.

There is also the critical problem of the asset specificity of the teachers. Putting teachers in an unrestricted market situation would threaten their knowledge and skills in various ways. According to transaction cost economics, such a situation is not stable. Either workers will demand high wages to compensate for their exposure or they will demand safeguards to protect their assets. (The New York City school decentralization reform of the 1960s in which schools were handed over to local control resulted in an extremely bitter dispute between community and parents on one side and the teachers' union on the other. Community groups wanted to replace teachers. Eventually, the teachers' union won after a long, destructive conflict.)

Perhaps the biggest difficulty with schools of choice is the asset specificity of the students. Market schemes presume that if parents and students don't like the school they are in, they can simply leave the school altogether, as customers might cease shopping at a particular mall. However, such an impersonal market prevails only where there is no asset specificity. Students actually develop a heavy investment in their school over a period of time. They invest in particular friendships, participate in particular social structures, learn from a particular curriculum that is sequential in nature, and so on. The investment in a particular school is very high, as anyone who has tried to get children to move or attend another school knows full well.

When parents first consider which school their children should attend, the situation resembles a market. However, once the investments begin the relationship quickly turns into one of bilateral dependency, similar to the bilateral contracting relationships analyzed before. Friendships develop, teachers come to know the students personally, including their personalities, learning styles, and parents. Everyone develops in-depth specific knowledge. Hence, withdrawing from the school because of poor performance of the school is not a viable option for most. Rather, in such asset-specific relationships, the parties to the contract will try to find special safeguards to protect their investments. So the mechanism of withdrawal and open competition will not work in the way stipulated by market advocates.

As it stands, Chubb and Moe's (1990) market reform proposal would seem severely deficient on recognizing asset specificity. People with asset-specific skills will not risk those assets in a free, impersonal market situation. Although correctly recognizing that decisions in education are bottom-heavy and performance is difficult to measure, the scheme also assumes too much ability on the part of students, parents, teachers, and schools to perform well once autonomy is given and parents' wishes are made known.

There is the provocative question raised by Chubb and Moe (1990) as to whether the problems of the school are caused by its democratization through an elected school board. In a review of research on politics at the local level, Iannaccone and Lutz (1994) contend that lack of change in local schools is caused by local constituencies that don't want the schools to change. When they do, they vote a change-oriented board into power. "The people can get what they want and, therefore, get what they deserve. The evidence of 30 years of research is clear. When voters in typical school districts become dissatisfied enough, they act" (p. 43).

On the other hand, in the largest cities, there is a question as to how democratic the school board is. The social class values and political rhetoric of officials and their clients do not mesh, the ethnic and cultural fit between the governors and those governed is nonexistent, and the ratio of representatives to voters is a sham (Iannaccone & Lutz, 1994, p. 47). Consequently, in large cities it *is* impossible to reform schools without changing school governance. Iannaccone and Lutz agree that governance has failed, but the failure is caused by not enough democratization rather than by too much. They agree with Chubb and Moe (1990) that schooling is too much in the hands of professionals and middle-class "progressives."

What might be gained by comparing school governance with contemporary corporate governance? Williamson (1985) suggests that shareholders, those who supply the corporation with equity financing, have put their assets at risk in the firm and risk appropriation without safeguards. The safeguard that arises endogenously is a governing board that is elected by shareholders and represents mostly their interests. This board can replace management, has access to performance measures, can authorize audits, is apprised of important proposals, and assumes a decision and monitoring role in general. Analogously, those who supply money for the operation of schools, the taxpayers, ideally should have representation on such a board. Who else?

Students and parents have huge investments in the school that they cannot easily withdraw without penalty. Chubb and Moe (1990) suggest that parent and student interests are not well served by school boards, and they may be correct. One can see how public members interested mostly in keeping spending low might starve the schools for money. Parents can only appeal to the board or try to penetrate a sometimes implacable bureaucracy. So parental interests might be represented directly on governing boards, along with taxpayer interests. In most schools student interests would be represented by parents.

To be sure, having parents on the governing board opens prospects of opportunism in which special constituencies demand special favors for their children.

There are also information costs associated with keeping board members informed. Participation should be limited to strategic levels of the organization, not the operational level. Given the nonrepresentiveness and unresponsiveness of large city school districts to constituencies, the benefits would seem worth the costs.

On the other hand, there is no compelling reason for putting teachers or administrators, contractors or suppliers, on the governing board (except for informational purposes). Their interests can be represented and negotiated in other ways. The more groups on a governing board, the more difficult performing duties becomes. A governing board consisting of many diverse interests often resorts to interest-group bargaining, as Chubb and Moe (1990) suggest.

## INFORMATION COSTS

The case for the market as superior because of its efficiency rests on certain assumptions (Buchanan, 1991):

- Full information is available about the performance and quality of goods and services, and the cost of this information is zero.
- Costs of enforcing contracts are zero.
- Individuals are instrumentally rational.
- Transaction costs are zero, including transportation and negotiation.
- There is perfect competition and no externalities (an effect not provided for in the contractual arrangement).
- Products in the market are undifferentiated, i.e., the buyer cannot distinguish among them.

When all these conditions are met, exchange will occur until a state of equilibrium is reached such that no one can be better off without making someone else worse off. However, these conditions are so stringent that they can never be met in actual markets. So the question is whether an actual market is beneficial, given that it cannot meet these theoretical criteria. The usual hope is that competition among producers over time will approximate these idealized conditions. The cost and availability of information are critical. In short, the information required of participants in market situations is minimal compared with that required by central planners.

Markets tend not to be efficient because of high transaction costs, lack of information on the part of producers and consumers, monopolistic tendencies, the presence of externalities, barriers to collective action to secure public goods the market cannot supply, lack of congruence between satisfaction of individual preferences and the individual's well-being, and unemployment (Buchanan, 1991). (Some market limitations will be considered later.)

In thinking about the privatization of schools, it is instructive to look at Stiglitz's (1994) analysis of why market socialism failed in eastern European countries. Stiglitz, a prominent economist and head of Clinton's economic advisors at one time, places a premium on the role of information in economic transactions. Under neoclassical economic theory the invisible hand of the market works well because there is perfect competition and perfect information. However, these two conditions almost never prevail in actual markets. And when these assumptions are not carried forward, market transactions take on quite a different character.

Market socialists thought they could have the benefits of a market economy even while the government owned the firms. In Stiglitz's (1994) view, the problem was that "price-taking" behavior associated with perfect competition and information is not how markets work. Government planners did not have the information required to run the economy. They could not specify the precise nature of every commodity, especially its quality. Specifications were set, and producers had incentives to meet the targets set for them at the lowest acceptable level. Hence, quality deteriorated. This substantiates Hayek's (1937) contention that the practical task of gathering the necessary information for central planning is beyond human capacity. (One is reminded of the Soviet ill-fated attempt to control production through performance indicators; see Pollit, 1990.)

To Stiglitz (1994) this is largely an information problem. If authorities had perfect information on each person, then proper work targets and rewards could be set. But obtaining such information is impossible. In general, inputs and effort are not observable. Outputs are not observable, or observable only through very imperfect indicators, so that it is impossible to know whether people are doing the right thing. In fact, what is the "right thing"? One way to control production in the face of such insufficient information is through work organized around an assembly line. Socialist countries did better at heavy industry than in service areas. But such monitoring is of little use in high technology. The most important characteristic of an economy is its ability to adapt to changing circumstances, especially in high-technology areas, and this the socialist economies lacked (Stiglitz, 1994).

In public-sector production these problems are compounded. There are multiple objectives, measuring outputs is problematic, measuring the contributions of individuals and suborganizations to the overall productivity of the firm is all but impossible, and even measuring inputs is difficult. One can measure time expended but how does one measure effort? Such information is not available for anything like reasonable cost. The private sector shares many of these information problems. In Stiglitz's (1994) analysis the deciding factor is not who owns the firm. However, the private sector is more efficient *on average* because competition in the public sector is weaker, the threat to the organization is less tangible; the government faces additional constraints, such as equity concerns, and difficulty making commitments, such as not to intervene.

Certainly education does not fit the standard assumptions of neoclassical markets either. "Consumers" are not perfectly informed or anything close to it. There are not large numbers of producers easily accessible. Financial incentives do not play a large role in the thinking of administrators or teachers. And output is very difficult to observe so mistakes and inefficiencies are difficult to detect. "Certainly scores on standardized tests do not even measure well such narrowly defined objectives as contributions to an individual's earning capacity (human capital)" (Stiglitz, 1994, p. 235).

However, although education does not meet these market assumptions, more interschool competition and choice would help, in Stiglitz's (1994) view. Contest, not perfect competition, is the essential ingredient. In imperfect information situations, without contests we don't know whether a firm is performing well or not, and contests can take place even where there are few firms. How we are to measure the outcomes of these contests, Stiglitz doesn't say. He recognizes that there are some negative effects of competition as well, such as raising a rival's costs, wasting money, and undervaluing cooperation.

In general, in his view the standard (neoclassical) market paradigm goes astray by overestimating the availability and underestimating the cost of acquiring information. It assumes that variables of interest are perfectly observable and that the employer can costlessly ascertain levels of effort and make payment contingent. Furthermore, the employee can be given instructions to do A or B, and individual discretion plays no role. In fact, communication among producers and users cannot be limited to price signals, and production is more a process of negotiation than of price-taking. In market socialism, "the central planner did not have to have all the information concerning preferences and technology. Communication between the central 'planners,' firms and households was mediated by the price mechanism. The 'messages' sent were fairly simple: Prices are sent, and quantity demands and supplies are given in response" (Stiglitz, 1994, p. 153).

One cannot help seeing similarities between this conception of market socialism and the application of national goals and standards to education. Central planners determine what schools are to teach and students learn; schools and teachers are supposed to meet these targets. In Stiglitz's (1994) view at least, it is precisely the inability of the government to make such determinations that caused the failure of market socialism. Government planners simply do not have the necessary information either to define the requisite skills or to monitor performance accurately when it occurs. So this is a strong case for decentralization, with or without private ownership.

Decentralization is motivated by the limited capacities of individuals and firms to process and transmit information. Individuals have limited ability to gather, absorb, and process information, and the ability of any centralized authority to gather, process, and disseminate information is also severely limited. Transmission of information is noisy and incomplete; error is common. However, decentralization can be achieved within government, as well as through privatization. The main case for privatization rests on the government's inability to make commitments, that is, *not* to intervene when they have the power to do so.

From this analysis one would think that education would not be well served by centralized management schemes, such as those that define goals and standards for schools to accomplish, that decentralization is necessary, that contest and choice are highly desirable, and that these could be accomplished through public as well as private means. Privatization serves primarily as a protector against government. Also, incentive schemes that attempt to measure the contribution of teachers or schools too precisely are ill conceived.

What I take from this discussion of markets in education is that decentralization is essential; that it can be accomplished within a properly run school district, but only one that has been totally recast to eliminate the large bureaucracy; that different schools must be created to compete with others; that the governance of the schools should be changed somewhat; and that this can probably be done through something like charter schools.

One underlying critical factor is the information available at the school and classroom level, which is a specific asset of local teachers. How can that information be improved? Although restricting the bureaucracy and encouraging new ideas are necessary steps, they are insufficient for productivity gains. They merely open the door of possibility. In the next chapter we turn to strategies for improving the teachers' specific information, on which so much depends. A school like Central Park East is one way to make this happen.

## REGULATED SCHOOL CHOICE

One of the strongest objections brought against school choice and voucher plans is that such educational markets would further extend the racial and socioeconomic segregation that already exists in many American school systems. Even though market plans might be good for some students, those who could take advantage, it would not be good for poor students or for society at large. It might create a more stratified, racially divided society.

Chubb and Moe (1990) don't deal with this objection, but most market advocates say that such plans would enable poor children and minorities to take benefit of choices or else that certain rules and regulations would have to be passed to prevent socially undesirable outcomes—for example, schools might be required to admit certain percentages of minorities. For their part, minority groups are opposed to market plans generally, for the reasons stipulated, though some might be in favor. For example, one could imagine all-black academies operating on

Afro-American principles, the way private Catholic or Jewish schools operate on their principles.

There is little empirical evidence to address what is likely to happen under market conditions. For the last several years New Zealand has had a free enterprise government, which has pursued very strong private-sector policies in education, as well as in almost every sector of the government (Boston et al., 1996; Kelsey, 1995). In 1991 New Zealand adopted a market education policy in which there were no school zones and in which schools were required to accept students unless the schools were overcrowded. Waslander and Thrupp (1995) have studied the effects of these policies on school enrollments and behavior in one city.

A complex pattern of school choice emerged. Over a 3-year period the percentage of students attending local (in-zone) schools dropped from 78% to 71%, those attending adjacent schools rose from 12% to 18%, and those attending distant schools requiring considerable travel remained the same at 11%. So nearby schools did provide some competition. Of course, most students did not change schools at all. The students who went to schools outside their zones tended to be from higher socioeconomic backgrounds than others. Across all schools socioeconomic and racial segregation increased, the two factors being confounded by occurring together (Waslander & Thrupp, 1995).

In case studies of four schools, the lowest income school with the most minorities lost the most students to the point where numbers of classes and teachers were reduced. The lowest SES students remained. To maintain itself this school tried various marketing schemes, such as brochures, new uniforms, a new disciplinary code, and hiring management consultants. The main academic reform was to retain students an extra year before the exams, which also increased enrollment. Overall, the school struggled to change its "image," albeit unsuccessfully.

The adjacent school into which numbers of minorities switched subsequently suffered "white flight" to yet other schools, thus increasing racial segregation. In trying to keep its white population, the school considered ability grouping, which they thought would appeal to white, middle-class parents, but such a move posed an ethical problem because the administrators and staff did not believe in "streaming" students in this fashion. They struggled to restore their old racial balance.

The local school with the best reputation quickly filled up (enrollment rose 12%), partly as a result of the trends at the other two schools. This school convinced the Ministry of Education that it was overcrowded and managed to get its target population reduced from a projected enrollment of 1,800 students to 1,080. This allowed the school to choose students the school wanted and also helped the schools suffering enrollment declines. This school's main objective was to be competitive with wealthy suburban schools, and to this end several classes were "streamed."

The wealthy, high-status suburban school saw no advantage in increasing its size. It was oversubscribed already by those wanting to attend. The Ministry of

Education ordered it to take more students, and it responded by giving preference to local (high SES) students, thus in effect maintaining its old zoning. It offered the same academic program it always had and felt no competitive pressure. So the result of this ambitious market scheme was not what policymakers anticipated (Waslander & Thrupp, 1995). The working-class schools were most affected, but the result was more racial and SES segregation. The schools affected tried to protect themselves by marketing to parents and considered academic changes that might satisfy parents. According to the researchers, it was difficult to see how educational performance was raised in any of the schools.

Herbert Gintis (1994), a neo-Marxist economist, advocates a school choice system in which the government regulates the educational market to some degree, as already happens in airlines, insurance, medicine, and so forth. In his view there is no reason to believe that governments are superior as producers of goods and services, as evidenced by the inefficiency of state-run industries, but, on the other hand, the government can regulate industries effectively. This asymmetry is due to governments' being unable to assess the relative performance of public-sector producers. After outlining ways in which an educational market might go astray, he proposes strong government regulation.

Frankly, however, it is difficult to see how governments can successfully regulate undesirable effects like racial and SES segregation, as the New Zealand policies indicate. There are many ways for schools and parents to avoid such regulation. After all, if governments cannot regulate racial segregation out of existence when the schools are under direct control, how likely is it that it can do so without such control?

My own view is that more varied schools with different offerings would be useful for reform efforts and that these might take the form of charter schools in which schools experiment with new forms freed of most regulations. Parents could be given more choice to send their children to other schools or to charter schools, under more supervision than a complete market system allows. Market organization of schools raises fundamental questions about schools in a democratic society. Should schools be organized for public purposes that are agreed to, or should they be organized by private individual purposes sorted out by markets?

## PERFORMANCE INCENTIVES

In *Making Schools Work*, Hanushek (1994) focuses more on the classroom than on governance mechanisms.

> If a single, glaring lesson is to be learned from past attempts at school reform, it is that the ability to improve academic performance using standard, uniformly applied policy is limited. . . . the most appropriate, indeed, the only place to begin promoting

diversity is at the basic unit of the school: the individual teacher in an individual classroom. (p. 85)

He goes on to say that it is impossible to define "best practice" among teachers because there is none. Teachers succeed and fail in many different ways. The reason decentralized management schemes have failed to improve education so far is that they lack clear incentives for teachers to improve. Improvement depends on individual teachers' being rewarded for good performance and punished for bad. This requires performance evaluation systems that are not simplistic. (Most teachers in elementary and secondary schools are paid according to years of experience in the school district and educational credits attained.)

One way to achieve this is through performance contracting (in which a contractor is paid according to results achieved), merit pay for teachers, and schools of choice. All these mechanisms have problems, in Hanushek's (1994) view. On schools of choice: "Because of limited experience with choice, little is known about whether choice will encourage development of new and innovative schools" (p. 107).

Instead, Hanushek proposes three broad principles: increasing the efficiency of resource use; using performance incentives; and learning from experience. Evaluation is critical to performance incentives. If one cannot accurately assess the performance of teachers, then how can one reward them for achievement? He insists on using student achievement measures for these evaluation purposes. He recognizes that student achievement is derived from many sources and that a performance-assessment mechanism must assign responsibility to teachers in proportion to what they have accomplished. They cannot be responsible for all student achievement because they are not the cause.

Unfortunately, Hanushek (1994) seriously underestimates the difficulty of measuring performance by standardized tests. There simply are no standardized tests available that measure student performance accurately and no way of parsing out the achievement attributable to individual teachers (Meyer, 1993). Such a technology does not exist, nor it is likely to exist soon. It would be possible to evaluate teacher performance using nonstandard methods that are not based on student test scores. Although Hanushek rejects such nonstandard methods, universities evaluate faculty performance in this fashion all the time.

Performance contracting involves writing a highly specific contract. The group is rewarded according to the terms of the contract and the results produced. Writing a contract is not easy, and so far the results have been disappointing where such an approach has been tried, as in the Baltimore and Hartford, Connecticut, schools and the Office of Economic Opportunity program in 1970. Mostly, there has been a failure to raise test scores or too much teaching to the test, which invalidates the payoff test.

I certainly agree about better resource allocation, especially in large city

FIGURE 9.1. Attributes of Educational Reforms II.

| Bounded Rationality | Opportunism | Asset Specificity | Reforms |
|---|---|---|---|
| ? | + | 0 | Open market |
| ? | + | 0 | Regulated market |
| ? | + | + | Charter schools |
| 0 | + | + | Incentives |

Note: A "+" indicates that the attribute is sufficiently considered; a "0" indicates that it is not sufficiently considered;and a "?" indicates that there is some question as to whether the attribute is sufficiently considered.

schools, and Hanushek's (1994) third principle, learning from experience, is well taken. He points out correctly that schools are not organized to learn from their environment. Learning is done by individual teachers. He suggests two strategies: systematic experimentation and evaluation, and improved student assessment. Although Hanushek underestimates the problems with research, evaluation, and testing, he is quite right in suggesting that these are not typically employed in school districts and could be much more useful than they are now. (Research-based and other learning strategies will be discussed in Chapter 10.) In general, the problem with performance incentives is that of information costs. The information needed is not available at anything like the cost that is affordable.

In summary, one could institute performance incentives and these would motivate teachers and administrators to do a better job. However, standardized means of performance assessment are lacking. In other words, there is bounded rationality not only on the part of teachers, which Hanushek recognizes, but also on the part of the measurement and evaluation research communities and the administrators who manage the school districts, which he does not recognize. These groups cannot supply the evaluation and assessment techniques needed, except perhaps at great cost. On the other hand, Hanushek's scheme recognizes the asset specificity of teachers (see Figure 9.1).

## CONCLUSION

Market reformers point to important problems with the schools. A huge unresponsive bureaucracy is the main one, and they propose making schools responsive to market forces, such as consumers, that is, the parents of students. Schools and teachers would be forced to be responsive to parents and students or they would go out of business because parents would send their children to other schools. Hence, reform would be forced on the schools as in the commercial marketplace.

However, education is not like a neoclassical market of impersonal buyers and sellers. Withdrawing one's child from school is not like shopping at another mall. Rather, the child has specific assets invested in the school in the form of relationships with friends and teachers. These are given up only with the greatest reluctance. Indeed, most such schemes have resulted in far fewer students' choosing alternatives than anticipated. The market resembles one of bilateral relationships in which people have heavy investments at risk. With specific assets at risk, they are likely to protect their assets in other ways. Teachers, for example, can be expected to protect their assets, the specific knowledge they have accumulated, by resisting strongly any market scheme that puts them at risk.

Nonetheless, what markets emphasize is that the necessary information to make things work is not available to central planning authorities. This is true for economies in general, and it is true for school districts and for state and national educational systems. As Chubb and Moe (1990) assert, education is a bottom-heavy technology in which decisions must be made at the school and classroom level because the proper information is not available elsewhere. This information involves knowledge of specific students and subject matter, and the context in which these interact. The understandings are too complex for simple information schemes to comprehend.

What seems reasonable in these circumstances is to introduce new ideas and competition by letting schools and teachers experiment with different ways of doing things. Schools of choice might provide competitive variety without expecting large numbers of students to migrate from school to school seeking the best bargain. Such variety is now lacking in centrally controlled school systems. Again, a multidivisional form of school governance with a small central staff might promote such opportunities, as well as try to ascertain their success.

# CHAPTER 10

# ASSET POLICIES: RESEARCH, SELF-ASSESSMENT, AND SMALL SCHOOLS

Teachers learn to teach through direct experience and participation. From direct experience they draw cause-and-effect inferences as to what works and doesn't work for them. This knowledge is personal and particular to the actual situation, and much of it is tacit: The teacher knows how to do things he or she cannot explain. Strategies for improving education must acknowledge this basic fact. One way to proceed is to increase the specific skill assets of teachers in some way.

## TEACHER INVOLVEMENT

If teaching technology is bottom-heavy, what about engaging the teachers in the work process in a different way? In reviewing the literature on employee involvement, Mohrman, Lawler, and Mohrman (1992) identify three basic approaches: parallel-suggestion involvement, job involvement, and high involvement. Parallel-suggestion involvement sets up parallel structures, like quality circles, for workers to make suggestions or monitor the organization. However, typically this involves only a small part of the work force, is difficult to maintain for long periods of time, and does not change the basic structure.

Job involvement focuses on redesigning work by job enrichment and establishing teams or work groups. Teams are particularly appropriate in process production where the technology depends on interdependent activity. These approaches have resulted in productivity improvements, higher quality, and lower turnover in industry, as well as reductions in supervision. On the other hand, they do not capture the contributions workers can make to higher-level decisions. Also, supervisors often make unilateral decisions that negate the effects, unless structural changes are made in management as well.

High involvement creates an organization in which workers care about the performance of the organization as a whole, are able to influence decisions, are rewarded for their contributions, and have the knowledge and skills to contribute. Rewards are based on the overall performance of the organization, perhaps through profit sharing or employee ownership. Workers have the appropriate knowledge, are committed to the organization, and are valued for their skills and contributions.

In deciding on appropriate employee involvement strategies, Mohrman, Lawler, and Mohrman (1992) suggest that the critical factors are the degree of interdependence of the work, the degree of complexity, and the amount of uncertainty. Educational work is high on all these factors. High interdependence argues for teamwork, while low interdependence argues for maximizing individual performance. Education is organized as if individual teacher productivity is all that is necessary.

However, one can make a strong case that teaching should be interdependent, for example, following a student through several years of schooling and outside the classroom to further his or her progress. Schools could be organized with teams of teachers managing groups of students. One reason for education's lack of improvement may be that it is improperly organized, given the requirements of the task. Another factor is the complexity of the work. Low complexity calls for simple job definition and incentive pay. High complexity calls for job enrichment at the individual or team level. Although many reforms assume low complexity, the reverse is more accurate for teaching.

> Teachers are required to simultaneously focus on the characteristics of the content that is being taught, diverse materials that are being used, the varying characteristics of the individual learners, the instructional processes, and the group processes that are established in the classroom. (Mohrman, Lawler, & Mohrman, 1992, p. 354)

Teaching is a complex job that requires balancing many simultaneous, interacting factors. High-involvement strategies are appropriate because individuals who are able to perform such work also possess the skills to contribute to higher-level decisions. Unfortunately, they are not allowed to do so in most educational settings.

A third factor is the amount of uncertainty inherent in the task, that is, the amount of on-line information processing required to know how best to do the job. Uncertain work involves discretion on the part of the worker, and teaching is very uncertain. Each student brings a unique set of personal and intellectual characteristics that must be understood and responded to by the teacher. Furthermore, these traits may change daily. Students' interaction with each other introduces yet more uncertainty. Teachers do not have control over many aspects of their job, which argues for involvement beyond the classroom. Collective approaches make sense.

Organizationally, high employee involvement calls for a flat administrative structure and for administrative units to be small enough that teachers feel they can influence them. Mohrman, Lawler, and Mohrman (1992) also argue that there must be mechanisms for clarifying desired outcomes and measuring them. Such mechanisms do not necessarily have to rely on stated goals. Finally, revolutionary improvement in performance can be attained only by making fundamental changes in the architecture of the organization. Significant change may require redesign, and, ideally, such change should result from processes in which workers participate.

Some strategies for improving the teacher's cognitive assets involve applying research findings in some fashion. Others involve redefining the job. Yet others recast the school as a whole so as to maximize teacher chances to learn about students and other teachers. In this chapter, I discuss research-based strategies, explore how evaluation of teaching might be changed, and conclude with a school redesign project, Central Park East, that emphasizes small school size as critical.

## RESEARCH-BASED STRATEGIES

Although teachers are more rational and effective than many believe, this does not mean that assistance from outside is unnecessary or undesirable. After 4 or 5 years of teaching, teachers often become set in their ways and less flexible than they once were, as we all do. This is partly a result of having mastered their craft. Routine, boredom, and inflexibility become problems in the careers of many. Change is necessary, as in any profession, even for the best teachers. If change occurs through individual teacher inference, it is likely to be very gradual. Teachers have quite different capacities for learning from their experience. Bounded rationality is a factor, and research is one way of providing new ideas. Generic research strategies include the following five.

*Technical Transfer.* The idea that we can discover a principle or technique that works in one place and simply apply it in another is deceptive. The orthodox theory of causation, the regularity theory, asserts that we can never discern causation directly but can know causation only through repetition of events, regular succession, and correlation. Once we discover a causal regularity or law, it will be repeated in other settings, if we only take care to specify the necessary conditions. Although correctly discerning causation is a difficult problem, the transfer of techniques from one setting to another is not difficult. Like causes produce like effects.

This technical-transfer model works reasonably well in physically based professions such as medicine, though even here there are difficulties. For example, individual susceptibility to drugs varies tremendously, and in a medical specialty like psychiatry, the certainty of like causes producing like effects evaporates quickly. In education this technical-transfer model does not work well at all. For example, in the federal program known as the "Follow Through" experiment, the variation in effects among sites of the same programs was nearly as great as the variation among the programs themselves. If like causes produce like effects, the same program should produce similar results, but often it does not.

There is good reason for this lack of standard effects. Teachers depend heavily on implicit, tacit knowledge that they have learned. Much of this knowledge is specific, based on highly particular interactions and understandings. Successful teachers operate at the level of teacher interaction with one particular student. What makes this student tick? How will she respond if I do this? Will her mother support me if I do this? Such knowledge is not susceptible to standardization.

Developers should not stop trying to develop new techniques. New curricula and models of teaching can serve as guideposts to what is possible, even when they are not implemented. What one cannot expect is that teachers will adopt these techniques in anything like the fashion their developers envision. Teachers already have strong working knowledge of their classroom, and changes must be mediated through that. In general, the technical-transfer model has not proved to be an effective strategy for changing schools.

*Study and Prescribe.* A related strategy is to study what teachers think and do, then prescribe ways they might improve. This presumes that we know how to improve what they are doing but has the advantage at least of actually finding out what they are doing and thinking first. Shavelson and Stern (1981) have summarized such research as exists on teacher judgments and have suggested the construction of a taxonomy of critical teacher decisions. For example, research shows that teachers group students by reading ability without seriously considering other possibilities. Researchers might try to map out the consequences of such a decision and suggest information that might lead to better decisions. We are a long way from being able to construct such a taxonomy.

*Practitioners as Exemplars.* Another strategy is to admit that practitioners know more about practice than do researchers and study the practitioners who are the best exemplars. Scriven (1985) has argued that we need a "practical" science in education rather than a theoretic one. Educational researchers should abandon attempts to discover underlying principles and take the discipline of evaluation as the paradigm for educational research.

This strategy is to identify a number of practitioners who are outstandingly successful at the task in question, analyze the distinctive features of their approach, then teach new or unsuccessful practitioners the "winning ways." The strategy assumes that the best practitioners have learned how to teach successfully and know far more than the most knowledgeable researchers. The research task is to abstract from practice and teach that to others. The question is whether good teaching is abstractable and generalizable in this way. If teachers learn through doing, must they relearn through doing as well? Are the cause-and-effect relationships simple enough to be taught in this manner?

*Vicarious Experience.* Yet another strategy is to accept both the idea that practitioners know what they are doing and also that they learn primarily from experience. Stake (1985) has suggested that researchers conduct studies that will provide *vicarious* experience to teachers in such a way that the new experience will combine with the old. The role of the researcher would be to aid practitioners in reaching new experiential understandings, which Stake calls naturalistic generalizations. The difference is that direct participation is the primary basis for practice rather than vicarious experience.

The researcher presents portrayals of actual teaching and learning problems in the words of the people involved. These data provide teachers with vicarious experiences that interact with existing naturalistic generalizations from previous experience. Presumably the vicarious experience leads to naturalistic generalizations on the part of the practitioner and to action. The question is whether vicarious experience is powerful enough to interact with prior direct experience. Does reading a novel change one's life?

*Action Research.* The most radical strategy in this progression is to turn the investigation of good practice over to teachers altogether, with some help from researchers. Practitioners would operate as individuals or in groups to define their problems and study them in their own schools. Action research acquired a bad reputation in the United States in the 1950s when it consisted of teaching teachers quantitative research methodology and expecting them to produce research studies. The studies lacked sufficient rigor by research standards. However, teacher research does not have to be a weak version of that done by researchers.

If one conceives the basis of teaching as personal cause-and-effect inferences that individual teachers derive from their own direct experience, then it makes good sense to test these inferences against data beyond oneself. Standard research methods are not very useful for this purpose. What would be useful would be to engage one's colleagues in checking one's inferences at the level of detail and particularity. One can imagine procedures by which this could be accomplished.

There is little such teacher research in the United States at this time. In a study of a medium-sized school district in Illinois, McTaggart (1985) found only 3 of approximately 900 teachers doing anything like this. Insufficient time and resources and strong external accountability pressures mitigate against reflective practice. More action research has been conducted in England (Elliott, 1980, 1988), Austria (Altrichter, Posch, & Somekh, B., 1993), and Australia (McTaggart, 1985).

The basis of all these strategies is that knowledge is sufficient to change practice. There is no account of opportunism in such strategies. Also, although research addresses the question of the bounded rationality of the teacher, what about the bounded rationality of researchers (or teachers as researchers) who are to produce such knowledge? Educational research results so far have been less than dramatic.

## SELF-ASSESSMENT

Short of redesigning the school, there are better ways of organizing some aspects of teaching. For example, consider evaluation of teaching. Evaluation of teaching as it is conducted is universally despised by teachers (Johnson, 1990). Teacher evaluation problems include the fact that evaluation systems are developed for reasons of accountability external to teachers and rarely used to improve practice. In addition, teaching is so complex that a multitude of relevant factors must be evaluated, making results difficult to interpret (Good & Mulryan, 1990).

Of course, it is difficult to find consistent factors that work in all or most situations. First, collecting data for teacher evaluation is expensive. Since teachers work behind closed doors, and student test performance is not a reliable indicator of teacher performance, great effort must be made to secure relevant information. This means evaluation for improving performance cannot occur too often or too routinely (Eraut, 1989). The costs are prohibitive. Second, the data generated should include data about the teacher's own performance, hence, that it be "self-evaluation" of some kind (Barber, 1990). Third, the evaluation should involve one's colleagues; it should be "collegial" (Burgess, 1989). Data about one's own performance is a powerful stimulus to improve, and evaluation that includes criticism from colleagues provides intellectual and emotional support. The teacher's colleagues are the most credible sources of information about professional activities and a powerful influence.

Holly (1989) has summarized the relationship between teacher evaluation and professional development. To further teacher development, a teacher evaluation scheme should be context-specific to the people and circumstances; ongoing and formative in its aims; flexible and evolutionary, in that there is continuity and direction; comprehensive and relational, in that there is an overall framework the teacher can make sense of; and personally and institutionally relevant.

Furthermore, a good evaluation scheme should improve professional practice through reflection; by bringing tacit knowledge to consciousness where it can be questioned; by removing isolation and enhancing communication; by promoting a professional culture; by enabling educators to learn from practice; by encouraging interpretations from broader perspectives; and by providing a sense of history and direction (Holly, 1989, p. 113).

These criteria take into account the asset specificity of the teacher's investment by building on the teacher's current knowledge. Teacher evaluation as practiced tends to be episodic, ahistorical, short-term, confused in purpose, individualistic rather than collegial, not based on practice, not grounded in larger interpretive frameworks, and not based on data about teachers and students in context.

One way to offer teachers the opportunity to become reflective and improve the quality of their work is through *self-assessment* (Barber, 1990; Lapan & Hays, 1992; Rogge, 1967). This process requires that teachers monitor selected aspects of their own instruction. A number of data-collection techniques can be used as the basis for self-assessment, including audio- or videotapes of classroom instruction or student conferencing, questionnaires or interviews administered to students, interviews administered by one teacher to another, and teacher logs and journals.

Self-assessment is best implemented as a collaborative effort where a few teachers meet and learn to collect data about their teaching and follow a protocol for discussing representations of their instruction. In a supportive setting teachers are encouraged to discuss their own teaching actions and reflect on how they might improve. As they examine their own data, they are guided by questions about the findings from other teachers. For example, a teacher might teach a lesson and record it on videotape. A small group of four or five colleagues would analyze the tape using observational schemes and/or criteria provided in advance.

Others might ask the focus teacher to study the feedback and make comments about the data's implications for subsequent instruction. This process of visiting and revisiting the data allows the teacher and group to reflect on differing interpretations. Using insights gained from the critique, the teacher could move again to the planning and acting phases. Each teacher in the group would become the focus teacher in turn.

Self-assessment can produce significant improvement. It is effective because it is adaptable to each teacher and his or her unique classroom circumstances. This process allows teachers to improve performance and develop a more complete teaching repertoire. Of course, not every teacher will succeed. Some will be too threatened to withstand peer critiques. In the current system, there is little peer analysis of classroom work.

Judged by the criteria of transaction cost economics, self-assessment does fairly well. Clearly, it takes account of asset specificity by investing in the teacher's abilities. On the other hand, it does not assume that teachers already know the best way to do things, but rather provides a process for learning how to do things better. The weak point is the reward structure. What would impel teachers to engage in such activities? Although there are intrinsic rewards in working with colleagues once the process starts, why begin? Why subject one's teaching to such evaluation?

In the current system a teacher's classroom is sacrosanct, and weak teachers can hardly be expected to volunteer. Hence, to make this reform work requires inducements or working only with volunteers. By itself, self-assessment is deficient on opportunism. Of course, improvement would be long and laborious, a gradual build-up of specific assets, since it would take years to improve each teacher's performance. On the other hand, there would be improved performance.

## CENTRAL PARK EAST—THE ECONOMIES OF SMALL SCALE

Another strategy is to change the school itself in order to maximize specific knowledge. Perhaps the best known school in the country is Central Park East (CPE) in District 4, East Harlem. Debbie Meier founded this "school of choice" as part of District 4's choice policy (Meier, 1995). Although the school exists in a poor, largely minority community, the school's graduates have a 90% college attendance rate, and the rate of retention is very high—only 5% of students move or transfer annually. The CPE program has expanded to include two other elementary schools and two high schools.

Meier's (1995) insights into reorganizing schools are illuminating. In her opinion, the key to the success of these schools is that they are small. Ideally, elementary schools should be 300 students and secondary schools no more than 400. This small size allows for experimentation over a period of time. "In schools, big doesn't work no matter how one slices the data . . . what big schools do is remind us that we don't count for a lot" (Meier, 1995, p. 107). In Meier's analysis small school size is critical for six reasons:

The faculty, parents, and students must find enough time for discussion and argument in order to reach consensus as to what the school shall do, and these discussions must be face-to-face. The agreement reached provides a vision for the school and one voluntarily entered. Through ongoing discussions, persuasion takes place, which results in change. Furthermore, teachers can think and work together collectively and collaboratively in a small group. The faculty operates as a committee of the whole. Such collaboration is essential if there is to be a strong school culture or ethos.

Faculty must be held accountable collectively to produce the overall school effect. This means they must have access to each other's work. The teacher work group must be small enough to allow this to happen, to visit each other's classes and engage in peer critique. This means no more than 20 teachers.

Above all, teachers must get to know the students and their work, the way individual students think. Students must get to know each other and the teachers. "At a school like CPESS [Central Park East Secondary Schools], the shyest and least engaged student would not have suffered the fate that the average big school student takes for granted" (Meier, 1995, p. 112). Every student is entitled to be in a school small enough that he or she can be known by name to every faculty member and known well by a few. This means classes no larger than 20.

Small schools promote personal safety, physical and mental. Teachers can know and respond to students who might be upset or on edge.

Accountability is a matter of access, not of monitoring. There is no need for cumbersome and largely invalid measurement systems to tell parents what's going on. They can come see, as can central administrators. Meier (1995) concedes the necessity of some monitoring data for central administration purposes, for example, the racial composition of the school.

Small schools immerse students in a school culture that adults have a role in shaping deliberately, rather than abandoning students to an autonomous peer culture shaped by the mass media. Schools should not absolve themselves of having a strong deliberate influence on students as part of socialization. Large schools have abdicated such responsibility.

To accomplish what it needs to, the school must have autonomy, which was the motivation for starting the school. It must control budget, staffing, scheduling, curriculum, and assessment. "It doesn't do us much good to know each other well if we can't use that knowledge" (Meier, 1995, p. 115). Autonomy is nonexistent in schools in most large cities. Meier admits that one significant disadvantage of small schools is that they are more vulnerable because of their more personal nature. Everyone is affected by everyone else in such a small community. Factionalism can become a problem.

The second essential feature of CPE is choice. "A call for small schools turns out to be intimately connected with a call for choice. Once we create small, self-chosen, and largely autonomous communities, we'll have to face the right of youngsters and their families to choose between them since no two will be alike" (Meier, 1995, p. 116). According to Meier, creating these successful school experiments in New York City would have been impossible without choice. Because CPE is a school of choice it was permitted to experiment with new ideas in a way that would never have been possible in a mandatory school. Various stakeholders would have vetoed change.

However, although parental choice was necessary, it was not an end in itself and did not create the school climate. Choice allowed the opportunity for change. Although other choice schools in District 4 designed by teachers had a high level of teacher energy, esprit, and sense of ownership, only the CPE schools tried out radically different pedagogies. Choice by itself may create closer bonds between parents, teachers, and students and a sense of membership, but it cannot create a different school. In Meier's (1995) opinion, choice may be the *only* way to experiment with new pedagogies. Mandated change results in unwilling, unready parents and professionals, as well as manipulation of data by ambitious administrators. Eventually the schools return to the status quo.

As for those who oppose choice on grounds of equality, Meier contends that Americans have long supported two levels of schooling based on social-class differentiation, whether the schools are private or public. Social class is the most important factor determining how schools work and what values they promote. Schools of choice don't change that, and they might provide poor students with better schools closer to what high socioeconomic students already obtain tucked away in private schools or affluent suburbs.

On the other hand, pure choice schemes are the wrong pursuit and are ultimately self-defeating.

> In the end, of course, the marketplace undermines the rationale for public funding. If we assume always the primacy of our private interests over our public ones we're not far away from claiming an absence of responsibility for the next generation by anyone but those directly interested—parents. Why should all citizens be expected to finance what is only a matter of individual private gain? (Meier, 1995, p. 79)

What about the program? In the elementary schools, the teachers are responsible for no more than 40 students a day and have the same students for 2 years. The schedule is very flexible and begins with a 2-hour interdisciplinary period before lunch. The guiding intellectual framework is provided by five "intellectual habits": concern for evidence (how do you know that?); viewpoint (who said it and why?); cause and effect (what led to it, and what else happened?); hypothesizing (what if, supposing that?); who cares?

In the high schools, during the last 2 years every student must complete the requirements of 14 different "portfolio" areas: literature, history, ethics, science, math, media, arts, community service, apprenticeship, autobiography, and so forth, and present 7 of these areas to a graduation committee for questioning and defense. The committee consists of two assigned faculty, an adult chosen by the student, and a student. The purpose of this method of assessment, similar to a doctoral oral, is to strengthen shared and publicly defensible standards. If students fail, they can try again. (The school has not been able to eliminate grades.) By contrast, Meier (1995) calls high-stakes objective test assessments "snake oil." Such testing leads to cheating, directly and indirectly. No testing system can ever entirely avoid it. "People cheat on eye tests if they need to" (p. 43).

Teachers need a framework that enables them to know their students well and acquiring such knowledge takes time and trust. Furthermore, there are 6 scheduled school hours per week for the teaching staff to meet together. Teachers are encouraged to visit each other's classes and give feedback. What this Central Park East school organization does is maximize everyone's chances to learn about each other, as well as to learn subject matter and skills. The framework for school development is at least as important as the program itself.

Perhaps the role of the principal in the school is underplayed in modest fashion by Debbie Meier. The principal is critical to school change. The principal must not only support the change but must be very activist in pursuing it. It is significant that even though Meier started out as a principal-teacher, not wanting to separate herself from her colleagues, eventually she became a full-time principal. The school principal may be one administrator who is necessary for the school to function well. There is an extensive literature on the role of the principal in school change (cf. Golding & Rallis, 1993; Weiss & Cambone, 1994).

The CPE reform attends to the critical features of the school as an organization. By being small enough that parents and teachers can talk through problems in face-to-face conversation, it allows everyone to build their specific assets, which are heavily vested in particular and personal knowledge. This personal knowledge is the accumulated wealth of the school. That's why the small size is critical. Furthermore, small size facilitates agreement and criticism among the faculty, a way to develop their knowledge further.

The school succeeds because teachers know the students well and vice versa. Everyone has a personal investment. The public nature of the exams requires teachers and students to expose their performance, a time for accountability and learning. Hence, the reform takes account of bounded rationality, opportunism, and asset specificity in a total package.

I am not suggesting that Meier and her teachers thought about things in this fashion. Surely, they did not. Rather they proceeded intuitively and experimentally, step-by-step. But in understanding how people think and behave—teachers, students, and parents—they took care of the organizational features I have raised, plus more that my appraisal scheme doesn't address. The implicit knowledge of the successful practitioner is more complete than any theory is likely to be.

Meier (1995) mentions that her ideas are similar to those underlying the one-room school house, and that at one time she fantasized about being a teacher in such a school. For a few years, in third and fourth grades, I attended two different one-room schools. And they do offer the personal attention and close communal feeling that Meier describes. I also experienced the shock of being thrust back into a city school and feeling devalued in such an impersonal environment. The number of students the teachers must deal with is a serious problem, amenable only to a reduction in class size.

The one-room school is a good experience if the teacher is good. The teacher knows not only the 15 to 18 students in her class but also the families of the students. In the old days she was likely to be a daughter from the community and even to live with a local family. The social ties were tight, often too tight for the teacher's personal development. If the teacher is a poor teacher, then students are stuck with her for many years. In city schools students go on to another teacher the next year, or in CPE, every two years. And in one-room schools there is no mechanism for improving teacher performance. Although the teacher receives community criticism, there is little chance for professional critique. Of course, professional critique is also lacking in larger schools since teachers operate autonomously in their classrooms.

An important idea not covered by my appraisal scheme is respect. Meier (1995) discusses how school districts, including school principals, routinely show disrespect to both teachers and students, demeaning them in a number of ways. Mostly, this is done by making teachers follow rules and regulations and not allowing them to make important decisions outside their classrooms. It was a search for autonomy as a professional that led Meier to start Central Park East and to make it a place in which mutual respect was important. She quotes Sarason (1990) on "the complete inability of educational reformers to examine the possibility that to create and sustain for children the conditions of productive growth without those conditions existing for educators is virtually impossible" (p. 147).

About educational reform generally, Meier (1995) is scathing. Americans remember a mythical past that didn't exist to which they compare the schools.

> And school practices have barely changed at all from when most Americans were young. Teachers are still telling and students still assume that remembering what they've been told is the road to success. . . . Schools offer a convenient target for blame during anxious times but what makes them such a *great* target is that they often willingly accept the attack in the hopes that the attention will lead to more resources. It's like the class bad boy, who keeps hoping that if he acts up he'll get the attention he needs. Unfortunately, it works the same way for both schools and kids. You get more attention, but usually not the right kind. (pp. 73, 74, emphasis in original)

## CONCLUSION

Central Park East is close to the complete package. That does not preclude the possibility of putting together several complementary reforms. For example, one might blend the advantages of self-assessment, strong in bounded rationality and asset specificity, with performance incentives, which are weak on bounded rationality but strong on opportunism and motivation. However, one can see problems that might result as well. If one tried to evaluate performance on the basis of data generated by self-assessment, that would corrupt the information. So there may be unproductive interactions among combined approaches.

Actually, improving education through these kinds of reforms is not new knowledge. Michael Fullan (1982) has put the case for teacher improvement well: "Educational change depends on what teachers do and think—it's as simple and complex as that" (p. 107). And Fullan has thoroughly reviewed the relevant research that has led to such a conclusion (Fullan, 1982; Fullan & Stiegelbauer, 1991). I also have a preference for reforms that improve teacher knowledge and skills, especially knowledge about their own performance.

In summary, my best reform strategy would focus on greatly reducing the

FIGURE 10.1. Attributes of Educational Reforms III.

| Bounded Rationality | Opportunism | Asset Specificity | Reforms |
|---|---|---|---|
| 0 | 0 | 0 | Utopian "high-tech" |
| 0 | 0 | + | National Goals |
| ? | 0 | + | National Standards |
| 0 | + | + | Standards–New York |
| + | 0 | + | Networks |
| 0 | 0 | + | Decentralization |
| 0 | ? | + | U-form hierarchy |
| + | + | + | M-form hierarchy |
| ? | + | 0 | Open market |
| ? | + | 0 | Regulated market |
| ? | + | + | Charter schools |
| 0 | + | + | Incentives |
| + | 0 | ? | Research |
| + | ? | + | Self-Assessment |
| + | + | + | Central Park East |

*Note*: A "+" indicates that the attribute is sufficiently considered; a "0" indicates that it is not sufficiently considered; and a "?" indicates that there is a question as to whether the attribute is sufficiently considered.

administrative hierarchy (a necessity), transforming the purpose and structure of the central staff to a small strategic staff, reducing the size of schools to 300 or 400 students, making schools relatively autonomous, providing opportunities for schools of choice, encouraging the internal flexibility of a Central Park East, and introducing self-assessment and action research. These reforms recognize the grass-roots technology that personalized education consists of, push decisions to the school and classroom levels, and enhance the specific knowledge and skills on which good education is based.

No doubt, reforming schools in this manner would be a long, laborious process. It would cost a large amount of money. Changing automobile production is expensive, and there is every reason to believe that changing education would be too. Of course, this is not a happy message to take to politicians who want major reforms without major costs. Increasing the productivity of an industry, an educational system, or a country is complex and costly, which is why we are more likely to cut costs than improve productivity. (See Figure 10.1.)

# THE LIMITS OF PRODUCTIVITY

A few months before my mother died in 1993, my son asked her for some advice. He was confused about what he wanted to do with his life. He thought maybe he should join the army to gain some time and perspective. I thought it might not be a bad idea, since he didn't know what he wanted to do. He was staying with my mother when her fatal cancer was discovered, and as he talked over the prospects with her, she told him *not* to join. "This country is not what it used to be," she said. "The people in power don't care how they use young men anymore."

I was stunned by this comment, considering the source. People of my mother's generation and social class have always been intensely patriotic, certainly including her. During World War II, not only did my uncles and other relatives go away to fight the war, my mother worked in a munitions plant, partly from necessity but also to support the war effort. She was devoutly religious and patriotic. For me, her advice was a remarkable indication of how much the country has changed in 50 years.

Perhaps her opinion would have been different if the country had been in danger. Or perhaps this was the feeling of a woman at the end of her life, though she displayed no negative feelings toward anything else in her final days, just quiet resignation. The fact that only 20% of the American people trust the federal government to do the right thing most of the time, down from 76% 30 years ago, suggests deep citizen alienation beyond my gentle and forgiving mother (Gore, 1993). The bonds of nation and society have been eroded severely. Vietnam, Watergate—formative events, no doubt, leading citizens to lose faith in the government's truthfulness and intentions. Are there deeper causes?

For a long time there have been signs of serious alienation among minority populations, acted out in various ways, and since at least the Oklahoma City bombing, signs of alienation among majority groups as well. One cannot help wondering about the long-term stability of advanced capitalism in the United States, whether it somehow undermines the conditions of its own success. After all, in spite of its great successes and lack of serious competitors, capitalism is a relatively new social system evolved over only the past 400 years (Braudel, 1981/ 1982/1984).

Many great economists, including Adam Smith, Joseph Schumpeter, and Karl Marx, of course, did not think capitalism could survive, albeit for different reasons (Heilbroner, 1993). Smith feared that "all the nobler parts of the human character may be in great measure obliterated and extinguished in the great body of people" (quoted in Heilbroner, 1993, p. 124). And Schumpeter (1942) said that "capitalism creates a rational frame of mind which, having destroyed the moral authority of so many other institutions, in the end turns against its own. . . . The bourgeois fortress thus becomes politically defenseless" (p. 143).

Alienation may simply indicate that the economic system hasn't been productive enough, since we know that wages for most Americans have been stagnant since the early 1970s. But why not change the leadership, rather than withdraw? There is a question of whether leaving citizens to contend with market forces may erode social ties. The "creative destructive force" of capitalism, in Schumpeter's (1942) term, may undermine itself by weakening family, church, and community. There is the possibility that the economic system lives off the social cultural system and exhausts it eventually.

Most of this book has proceeded from a framework of economic productivity. I have tried to show that most plans for educational reform do not work well within such a framework. The incentives are wrong, the information inadequate, cognitive investments underappreciated—if one accepts that teacher and student behaviors "are rational responses to a calculus of expected costs and benefits" (Becker, 1993, p. 17). However, taking an economic perspective does not mean that other aspects of human nature are unimportant. What does such a framework omit, and what are the consequences of formulating and implementing policies that hew to such a narrow line?

## MARKET DEMOCRACY

The dominant market theory of democracy was first stated by Joseph Schumpeter (1942), and extended by Dahl (1956) and other leading political theorists. (For ways in which economic concepts have strongly influenced political theory, see Barry & Hardin, 1982; Boyd et al., 1994; Heap, Hollis, Lyons, Sugden, & Weale, 1992; and Wong, 1994.) In this model, democracy is simply a mechanism for choosing governments, and the mechanism consists of political parties competing with each other by presenting policies among which voters choose, as consumers do in a marketplace. Politicians are entrepreneurs selling ideas to the public.

Schumpeter (1942) quotes a prominent politician: "What businessmen do not understand is that exactly as they are dealing in oil so I am dealing in votes" (p. 285). And Schumpeter continues,

> But the department store cannot be defined in terms of its brands and a party cannot be defined in terms of its principles. . . . The psycho-technics of party management and party advertising, slogans and marching tunes, are not accessories. They are the essence of politics. . . . Party and machine politicians are simply the response to the fact that the electoral mass is incapable of action other than a stampede." (p. 283)

In his view, the public will is a "manufactured" will, constructed by those who control the publicity mechanisms. As he notes, this does not prevent individual politicians from embracing noble principles. However, one might add, neither does it encourage principled behavior. Such marketing results in a cynical view of democratic politics, expressed fully by Edelman (1964, 1988), who sees democratic politics as primarily symbolic rather than substantive. Even critics of this model of democracy acknowledge that it describes how things work currently.

Macpherson (1973, 1977, 1987) has called this version of democracy the pluralist-elitist-equilibrium model. It is pluralist in that society consists of many individuals and groups pulling in different directions. It is elitist because negotiations and compromises are carried out by leaders representing different interest groups, and the process maintains an equilibrium between the supply and demand of political goods. Critics like Macpherson have argued that only groups that have "purchasing power" have their preferences enacted. Money makes the difference. And some, like Lasch (1995), contend that the governing elites have abandoned any sense of public obligation whatsoever and now pursue solely their own welfare.

Politicians cynically construct policy platforms that appeal to the position that will elicit the most votes, resulting in blurred rather than clearly defined issues. Voters feel they have little to choose from. Following the logic of the market this results in an oligopolistic situation in which there are only a few sellers (parties) and relatively few buyers with money. "Demand" is generated not by the public at large but by powerful groups. Such a process eventually results in apathy on the part of an ineffective electorate, which believes that participation makes no difference.

Since Macpherson's (1977) critique, "think tanks" have emerged as the main suppliers of policies. Policy supply has become professionalized and heavily sponsored. Policies do not spring from unbiased origins and do not result in unbiased recommendations. If there were a free market of ideas, then presumably the market would select the best. However, entry into the market is not open or cheap, so that some ideas have tremendous advantages, particularly those amplified by the media. Policy entrepreneurs simplify their ideas into slogans to garner public support (Krugman, 1994b). The result has not been good economic or educational policy.

Although Lincoln's admonition that one cannot fool all the people all the time may be true, Schumpeter (1942) points out that most politics and policies are enacted over short periods of time, and the course of events may be changed irremediably by short-term actions, regardless of long-term consequences. In addition to transaction costs (the difficulty of participating in a remote government), lack of information (misinformed voters), and monopolistic tendencies (vested interests), there are other ways in which political markets can go wrong. They can produce externalities, fail to provide essential public goods, and satisfy individual preferences even while not providing for individual well-being (Buchanan, 1991).

Externalities include such things as pollution and congestion. But a positive externality like education, which produces benefits even for those who don't pay for it, may be underproduced because many benefit without paying. When a public good can be produced only with the cooperation of others, when benefits are available to all, when there is no practical way to prevent noncontributors from partaking of the benefits, and when the individual's contribution entails significant costs, conditions are ripe for *not* supplying the good (Buchanan, 1991). Free riders can benefit without contributing and may reason that someone else will pick up the tab. Hence, a valuable social good like education may be underproduced.

Another problem with markets, including political markets, is that giving people what they want may not contribute to their welfare. Individuals can be mistaken about their personal welfare (e.g., cigarette smokers). Of course, to give them what they "need" as opposed to what they "want" raises questions about paternalistic government deciding what's best. Nonetheless, in spite of the dangers of government intervention, there is a difference between needs and wants. Market advocates might retort that even though the market is an imperfect way of achieving the public good, it is better than the alternatives, including government intervention.

Some have proposed a different approach to democracy in which a deliberative or cognitive role would be played by new institutions (Hurley, 1989). Instead of satisfaction of individual preferences, which does not require careful consideration of issues, institutional devices to promote discourse, dialogue, and debate might be employed to arrive at better founded policies and prevent false beliefs from being propagated. However, such ideas are far from implementation or even adequate conceptualization. In fact, things seem to be moving the other way, toward television slogans.

## MARKET SOCIETY AND HUMAN NATURE

Finally, there is a fundamental question about the kind of person and society entailed by market societies. Transaction cost economists realize that their framework is "crude, instrumentalist, and incomplete" as an explanation of human nature.

As with economic models more generally, the human agents who populate transaction cost economics are highly calculative. That is plainly not an attractive or even an accurate view of human nature. Economics is thought to be a dismal science partly for that reason. But insistence on rationality is also the great strength of economics. . . . To be sure, rationality can be and sometime is overdone. Hyperrationality is mainly a fiction and/or a pathology. But one does not need to assert that the only reliable human motive is avarice to recognize that much of the success of economics in relation to the other social sciences occurs because calculativeness is presumed to be present in nontrivial degree. (Williamson, 1985, p. 391)

One can distinguish between *homo economicus* and *homo sociologicus* (Heap et al., 1992). *Homo economicus* is an instrumentally rational calculating seeker of preference satisfaction, a maximizer of utility, acting on personal preferences to attain his or her own ends. The theory of individual rational choice assumes that individuals have a set of objectives arranged in a preference ordering, and the task is to satisfy these objectives through action. Rationality reduces to the best means to the end, and the end of the economic agent is maximizing private interests (Little, 1991).

*Homo sociologicus,* by contrast, lives according to rules, roles, and relations, and thinks in terms of social norms and collective interests rather than individual preferences. Without doubt, there is truth in both portrayals of human nature.

The essence of liberalism . . . is the vision of society as made up of independent, autonomous units who co-operate only when the terms of co-operation are such as make it further the ends of each of the parties. Market relations are the paradigm of such co-operation. . . . To reduce it to dyadic terms, A will do what B wants (i) because B has authority over A (hierarchy), (ii) because B makes it worth A's while to do it (liberalism) or (iii) because A wants to help B (altruistic collaboration). (Barry, 1973, pp. 166–167)

Economists themselves have raised questions about the long-term effects of market societies. Competition is positive, but what about excessive competition? Does it extinguish cooperation? What happens when people pursue only their own interests? Does this destroy trust? Capitalism flourishes best with a combination of self-interested behavior and non–self-interestedness, where business can be conducted on one's word. If there is no trust, even the cost of doing business goes up enormously (Stiglitz, 1994).

Another economist has raised questions about the fruits of an ever-expanding economy (Hirsch, 1982). It is one thing to have a cottage on a mountain lake, but what about when everyone else also has a cottage on the same lake? As advanced capitalism moves past providing primary goods, it produces goods like cars and education, the value of which may be reduced by other people's possessing the same goods en masse. As the level of consumption rises, satisfaction depends increasingly on consumption by others as well. This is a recipe for mass frustration.

Education viewed as providing access to the most desirable jobs means that the utility of expenditure for education will decline as more people attain that level of education. In addition to an absolute sense of the quality of education (knowledge and skills attained), there is also a relative sense in which quality means one's differential over that attained by others. Not everyone can benefit in this second sense. Distributional issues become important. Individual pursuits are altered by their social consequences.

> In brief, the principle of self-interest is incomplete as a social organizing device. It operates effectively only in tandem with some supporting social principle. This fundamental characteristic of economic liberalism, which was largely taken for granted by Adam Smith and John Stuart Mill in their different ways, has been lost sight of by modern protagonists. . . . The attempt has been made to erect an increasingly explicit social organization without a supporting social morality. The result has been a structural strain on both the market mechanism and the political mechanism designed to regulate and supplement it. In this way, the foundations of the market system have been weakened, while its general behavioral norm of acting on the criterion of self-interest has won ever-widening acceptance. . . . A system that depends for its success on a heritage that it undermines cannot be sustained on the record of its bountiful fruits. (Hirsch, 1982, p. 169)

Reflecting on British society, Marquand (1988) locates the root of its problems in an individualist society operating without principles.

> Just as the world is made up of solid lumps of matter, so a society is made up of separate, sovereign, atomistic individuals. The obligations which these individuals owe to their society derive ultimately from the fact that it can be shown that it is to their advantage to belong to it. (p. 213)

> The polity is and can only be an arena for the pursuit of interests—of individual interests in the case of the neoliberals and of class interests in the case of the neo-socialists. For both, those interests are given; the products of prior individual preference or objective class situation, and therefore not subject to change by argument or debate. (p. 67)

Such a society will never survive in the long term, in Marquand's (1988) view. Citizens must be capable of rising above their own particular interests in order to make disinterested judgments of the general interest. Some sense of principle is needed. Appealing to calculative rationality alone is not enough in the long run. Amartya Sen (1987) says that running an organization purely on incentives to personal gain is hopeless. "The purely economic man is indeed close to being a moron" (p. 99). "Why should it be uniquely rational to pursue one's interests to the exclusion of everything else? (Sen, 1987, p. 15). Human beings are motivated by self-interest but also by altruism, among other things (Little, 1991).

> The concept of rationality is pressed into service . . . to plug the gap left by the absence or weakness of social institutions of the more traditional kind. It is scarcely surprising that it fails. Societies cannot, any more than individuals, tug themselves up by their own bootstraps. (Barry & Hardin, 1982, p. 370)

It is a good bet that in the future there will be a great deal of effort to establish some kind of moral enterprise, code, or institution that will govern relationships among people, in addition to market/contractual relations. The strong push toward values, character education, and religious fundamentalism of the political right, whether it be the Moral Majority, the Christian Coalition, or the Promise Keepers, is more than a passing reaction. It is a call for a politics of substance rather than procedure. Take a look at the faces at the rallies. They are young faces. (For an analysis of conservative movements in education, see Apple & Oliver, 1995.)

The communitarian movement in all its political and philosophical manifestations is another instance. The political left has not yet recovered from the conversion of the socialist countries to capitalism, but they will attempt to fill this moral gap eventually as well. Heilbroner (1993) notes that capitalism's uniqueness in history is its continuously self-generated change, but that this very dynamism is its chief enemy. There is a line across which other elements take precedence.

> The economy has dominated the polity in capitalist history to an extent unimaginable in previous regimes. Nonetheless, in our times we hardly need to be reminded of the latent powers that lie within the political realm. . . . We would then witness an assertion of national identity in defiance of economic trends, very likely by the formation of semi-autarchic national groupings. The logic of economics, which has guided so much of modern history, will then be edged aside—although I am sure not displaced—by that of politics. And what is the logic of politics? One suspects it will have to be learned the hard way. (pp. 82–83)

It will be another, later generation, probably my son's and daughter's, that will construct a new belief system that has appeal to vast numbers of people. The liberal theorists of the left, center, and right will give way to new thoughts, new thinkers, and new policies. From which direction they will come, I don't know, but they certainly will have strong moral content, not accounted for in current market conceptions, valuable as those may be. Like all truths, they are partial truths.

## MATCHING POLICY AND PRACTICE: A SUMMARY

National and state leaders formulate educational policies primarily in response to economic concerns without sufficient understanding or appreciation of educational institutions. This overdrawn focus causes educational policies to be mismatched to practices. Policies intended to increase productivity often decrease it. Nor do government leaders do this deliberately. Rather they are mistaken in their initiatives because they are misinformed and too far removed from educational work. Thus, educational policies dissolve into ineffectiveness, to be replaced by other ineffective policies.

There are four ways in which economic concerns influence educational policies. First, economic policies and conditions influence educational policies. Second, educational policies are formulated to reduce costs and increase the productivity of schools. Third, education and economic development are presumed to be closely linked. It is assumed that more or better education leads to improved technological capabilities and better jobs. Fourth, economic concepts have permeated educational thinking. Attendant to these influences are four types of errors: misunderstanding the economic system; misunderstanding the educational system; misunderstanding the fit between the two; and misapplying economic concepts.

For example, the economic policies of the Reagan administration, of simultaneously reducing taxes and greatly increasing military expenditures, thereby incurring a huge national debt, shifted large sums of money from the poor and middle classes to the wealthy and eroded the international economic position of the United States. The schools were blamed for many of the consequences, and the steadfast liberal belief that economic productivity depends on improving basic skills led educators to accept the blame. Conservatives pointed to undisciplined students, teachers, and workers as sources of the problems.

Educational policies of the 1980s were attempts by federal, state, and local governments to deal with the ensuing crises by disciplining students and teachers through tougher regulations and standards, by adding requirements and achievement testing, and by intensifying competition among students and organizations. Other reforms, such as decentralization and schools of choice, attempted to change the basis of school governance. The reforms had in common that they cost little, were meant to discipline students, and protected the interests of the middle and upper classes.

On entering office, Clinton was limited in what he could do by budget and economic conditions. Room for maneuver came in developing national standards and national tests. A related initiative was systemic reform, with states developing curriculum frameworks, standards, and tests. These ideas do not cost much new money. Establishing tight systemic connections among all these elements seems unlikely because of many difficulties, not the least of which are conflicting goals and interests.

The United States does face a serious economic problem. Its productivity rate has declined over the past decades, which translates into a lower standard of living. The reasons for this include lack of investment in R&D, short-term business management, bureaucratization of large firms, and slowness in adopting revolutionary production techniques. Education plays a modest role. Although "strategic traders" contend that solutions lie in improving international competitiveness and "supply siders" advocate cutting taxes and regulations, no one fully understands why productivity has declined or how to remedy it. The problem seems to lie in the domestic service sector.

Similarly, productivity problems in education have little to do with what other countries are doing. The real problem is to increase the productivity of American schools by focusing on how teaching and learning are organized. Furthermore, education's role in the economy is complex. The idea that education leads to a better job and economy is too simple. Jobs require certain kinds of knowledge, and people learn this knowledge when the jobs are there. In a sense, the jobs precede the education. In the near future, many jobs will not require more education. Corporations might import educated workers or place jobs in other countries where workers already have a high degree of education rather than support an expensive education system.

Clinton and Gore also attempted to reform the federal bureaucracy to make it more like business. Managerial reforms included contracting out services, entrepreneurialism, performance indicators, and so forth. The checks and balances of the American system impeded implementation. However, the problems with market reforms in government run deeper. Markets do not work the same way in the public as in the private sector. Few buyers and few sellers result in "imperfect markets," which function in a different manner than neoclassical markets, which have many impersonal buyers and sellers. In such imperfect markets, transaction costs are high.

One way of regarding these reforms is to see them as the intrusion of inappropriate business ideas into the public sector. Another perspective is to regard them as a new form of government management. Bureaucratic control (centralization, formalization, specialization, and hierarchy) and professional control (collegiality, credentialism, self-regulation, semi-autonomy) seem to be giving way to postbureaucratic control (devolved control, regulated autonomy, decentralized centralism) based on horizontal contractual relationships.

Part II of this book dealt with contractual relationships in pursuit of school reform. Currently, schools are organized to produce educational achievement through blackboards, lectures, and seat work. This is an old-fashioned technology, though critics underestimate its effectiveness. Historically, it has done remarkable things for a low price per student. Nonetheless, if one wants significant improvements, there must be new arrangements. The difficulties of achieving such transformations are formidable, including costs for development, implementation, retraining, and information procurement, all of which are underestimated by reformers.

One might conceive of reforming schools as a contract between reformers and those who must undertake the reforms—the teachers, students, administrators, and parents. Transaction cost economics provides an analysis of such contractual relationships based on the attributes one ascribes to the parties to the contract. The three critical attributes of participants are bounded rationality (people have limited cognitive abilities), opportunism (people work for their own self-interests), and specific assets (people accrue valuable assets they cannot easily transfer elsewhere).

Teachers and students are bounded in their rationality, opportunistic some of the time, and accrue certain assets, especially cognitive assets. They are not particularly altruistic, rationalistic, or recalcitrant. They are willing to make investments as rational responses to expected costs and benefits. Perhaps least understood are the teachers' specific assets. For the most part, teachers learn to teach in the classroom on their own, which may take years. The knowledge of how to teach is mostly tacit and context-specific: what to do with these students in this place with this subject matter. When this knowledge of how to do things is threatened, teachers protect their investment.

Educational reforms can be appraised using the transaction cost criteria to see if the three critical attributes are sufficiently considered. National goals lack appreciation of opportunism and bounded rationality. Why should teachers pursue distant goals? Would they know how to accomplish these goals if they did? National standards also ignore opportunism and bounded rationality. Attempts to closely monitor teachers by using tests for accountability have resulted in distorted information. On the other hand, these reforms do acknowledge the specific assets of teachers.

Decentralization by itself ignores bounded rationality and opportunism as well. Just because an administrative structure is decentralized doesn't mean that teachers and administrators will know what to do. Decentralization is a necessary step toward effective school reform, but not sufficient in itself. The cumbersome administrative structures of school districts are serious impediments to change, and the solution might be to develop a multidivisional form of organizational structure so that a small central staff removed from daily operations plans the strategy of the organization, allocates money, and monitors performance, leaving operational decisions at the local level. This allows the school opportunities to change and the central administration opportunity to start new enterprises.

Market reforms propose making schools responsive to market forces. Schools and teachers would be forced to respond to parents and students or they would go out of business because parents would send their children to other schools. However, education is not a neoclassical market of impersonal buyers and sellers. Rather, each child has specific assets invested in the school in the form of relationships with friends and teachers. These are abandoned only with great reluctance. This market is one of bilateral relationships in which people have heavy investments at risk, and they are likely to protect their assets. Teachers can be expected to protect the specific knowledge they have by resisting market schemes that put them at risk.

Market advocates correctly stress that the information necessary to make things work is not available to central planning authorities. This is true for national economies and for education systems. Education is a bottom-heavy technology in which decisions must be made at the school and classroom level because the critical information is not available elsewhere. The required information is too complex for centralized data-collection systems to capture.

What seems reasonable in such situations is to introduce new ideas and competition by letting schools and teachers experiment with different ways of doing things. Charter schools might provide competitive variety without expecting large numbers of students to migrate from school to school seeking the best bargains. Again, a multidivisional form of school governance with a small central staff might promote such opportunities without hands-on control.

Asset-improvement strategies include different ways of using educational research and self-assessment of teacher performance. These build on the teacher's specific assets, though they lack control over opportunism. Another possibility is to combine complementary reform ideas. Successful reforms are likely to be highly complex in operation.

In sum, the best reform strategy would focus on reducing the administrative hierarchy, transforming the purpose and structure of the central staff to a small strategic staff, reducing the size of schools to 300 or 400 students, making schools relatively autonomous, providing opportunities for schools of choice, encouraging the internal flexibility of a Central Park East, and introducing reforms such as self-assessment and action research. These reforms recognize the grassroots technology that personalized education consists of, push decisions to the proper levels, and enhance the specific knowledge and skills on which good education is based. No doubt, reforming schools would be a long, laborious process costing a large amount of money.

If one were to develop a more complete appraisal scheme, one would have to take account of other important factors as well. It has been suggested that research on educational reform occurs from three basic perspectives—technological, political, and cultural (House, 1981). In a sense, transaction cost economics is an updating of the technological perspective. Political factors, such as conflicting interests, and cultural factors, such as the organizational culture, would expand the comprehensiveness of the appraisal scheme, as well as make it more complex. Nonetheless, all three perspectives are needed to understand and portray educational change.

The three basic perspectives rest on concepts drawn from economics, political science, and anthropology. Since disciplinary knowledge is abstracted from the institutions under study, such knowledge can never fully explain institutional reality, any more than physics can map every physical event. Combining all three perspectives would provide a more complete picture, but a picture still necessarily incomplete (House & McQuillan, 1997). The most that conceptual schemes can provide is a rough map of reality, hopefully one that identifies critical features.

They cannot substitute for reality. It is one thing to analyze educational reform and quite another to do it.

Finally, one might raise concerns about an educational system or a democracy based entirely on market principles and a rationality of calculative self-interest, which require eternal increases in productivity. Are such enterprises self-sustaining over a long period of time? There are some reasons to believe the answer is no. As the traditional institutions of society erode under market forces, alienation has become a major problem in advanced capitalist societies like the United States. Even leading economists doubt that these losses of stable social relationships can be compensated by increasing material prosperity indefinitely.

# REFERENCES

Altrichter, H., Posch, P., & Somekh, B. (1993). *Teachers investigate their work—An introduction to the methods of action research.* London/New York: Routledge.

Apple, M., & Oliver, A. (1995). Becoming right: Education and the formation of conservative movements. Madison: University of Wisconsin.

Apple, M., & Weiss, L. (Eds.). (1983). *Ideology and practice in schooling.* Philadelphia: Temple University Press.

Applebome, P. (1995, February 20). Employers wary of school system. *New York Times,* p. 1.

Astuto, T. A., & Clark, D. L. (1986). *The effects of federal education policy changes on policy and program development in state agencies and local education agencies.* Bloomington, IN: Policy Studies Center.

Baker, E., & Linn, R. (1993/94). Towards an understanding of performance standards. *The CRESST Line.* Los Angeles: National Center for Research on Evaluation, Standards, and Student Testing, UCLA.

Ban, C. (1995). Unions, management, and the NPR. In D. F. Kettl & J. Dilulio (Eds.), *Inside the reinvention machine* (pp. 131–151). Washington, DC: Brookings Institution.

Barber, L. W. (1990). Self-assessment. In J. Millman & L. Darling-Hammond (Eds.), *The new handbook of teacher evaluation* (pp. 216–228). Newbury Park, CA: Sage Publications.

Barberis, P., & May, T. (1993). *Government, industry, and political economy.* Buckingham, UK: Open University Press.

Barry, B. (1973). *The liberal theory of justice.* Oxford, UK: Oxford University Press.

Barry, B., & Hardin, R. (1982). *Rational man and irrational society?* Beverly Hills, CA: Sage Publications.

Becker, G. S. (1993). *Human capital* (3rd ed.). Chicago: University of Chicago Press.

Bell, T. H. (1988). *The thirteenth man: A Reagan cabinet memoir.* New York: Free Press.

Bergmann, B. R. (1986). *The economic emergence of women.* New York: Basic Books.

Bering, K. (1993, August 27–29). Germany to cut spending on R&D, alarming some. *Colorado Daily.*

Berlin, G., & Sum, A. (1988). *Toward a more perfect union: basic skills, poor families, and our economic future.* New York: Ford Foundation.

Berliner, D. C., & Biddle, B. J. (1995). *The manufacured crisis.* Reading, MA: Addison Wesley.

Bloom, A. (1987). *The closing of the American mind.* New York: Simon and Schuster.

Boston, J. (1994). Purchasing policy advice: The limits to contracting out. *Governance, 7*(1), 1–30.

Boston, J., Martin, J., Pallot, J., & Walsh, P. (1996). *Public management: The New Zealand model.* Auckland, NZ: Oxford University Press.

Bowles, S., & Gintis, H. (1976). *Schooling in capitalist America.* New York: Basic Books.

Boyd, W. L., Crowson, R. L., & van Geel, T. (1994). Rational choice theory and the politics of education: Promise and limitations. *Journal of Education Policy, 9*(5&6), 127–145.

Boyd, W. L., & Kerchner, C. T. (1988). (Eds.). Introduction and overview. In *The politics of excellence and choice in education* (pp. 1–11). London: Falmer Press.

Bradsher, K. (1995, August 28). Skilled workers watch their jobs migrate overseas. *New York Times,* p. 1.

Braybooke, D., & Lindblom, C. E. (1970). *A strategy of decision.* New York: Free Press.

Braudel, F. (1981/1982/1984). *Civilization and capitalism: 15th–18th centuries* (3 vols.). New York: Harper and Row.

Buchanan, A. (1991). Efficiency arguments for and against the market. In J. Arthur & W. H. Shaw (Eds.), *Justice and economic distribution* (pp. 184–197). Englewood Cliffs, NJ: Prentice Hall.

Burgess, R. G. (1989). A problem in search of a method or a method in search of a problem? A critique of teacher appraisal. In H. Simons & J. Elliott (Eds.), *Rethinking appraisal and assessment* (pp. 24–35). Buckingham, UK: Open University Press.

Burton, N. W., & Jones, L. V. (1982). Recent trends in achievement levels of black and white youth. *Educational Researcher, 11*(4), 10–14.

Callahan, R. E. (1962). *Education and the cult of efficiency.* Chicago: University of Chicago Press.

Carnoy, M. (1993). Multi-nationals in a changing world economy: Whither the nation-state? In M. Carnoy, M. Castells, S. S. Cohen, & F. H. Cardoso (Eds.). *The new global economy in the information age* (pp. 45–96). University Park, PA: Penn State University Press.

Carnoy, M., & Levin, H. M. (1985). *Schooling and work in the democratic state.* Stanford, CA: Stanford University Press.

Carroll, J. B. (1987, February). The National Assessment in reading: Are we misreading the findings? *Phi Delta Kappan,* 233–240.

Castells, M. (1993). The informational economy and the new international division of labor. In M. Carnoy, M. Castells, S. S. Cohen, & F. H. Cardoso (Eds.). *The new global economy in the information age* (pp. 15–43). University Park, PA: Penn State University Press.

Celis, W., 3rd. (1994, March 30). New education legislation defines federal role in nation's classrooms. *New York Times,* p. B7.

Chubb, J. E. (1988). Why the current wave of school reform will fail. *Public Interest, 90,* 28–49.

Chubb, J. E., & Moe, T. M. (1990). *Politics, markets, and America's schools.* Washington, DC: Brookings Institution.

Cibulka, J. G. (1991). Educational accountability reforms: Performance information and political power. In S. Fuhrman & B. Malen (Eds.), *The politics of curriculum and testing* (pp. 181–202). London: Falmer Press.

Clark, D. L., & Astuto, T. A. (1990). The disjunction of federal education policy and educational needs in the 1990s. In D. A. Mitchell & M. E. Goertz (Eds.), *Education politics for the new century* (pp. 11–15). London: Falmer Press.

Clune, W. H. (1993). Systemic educational policy: A conceptual framework. In S. H. Fuhrman (Ed.), *Designing coherent education policy* (pp. 125–140). San Francisco: Jossey-Bass.

Clune, W. H. (1993). The best path to systemic educational policy: Standard/centralized or differentiated/decentralized? *Educational Evaluation and Policy Analysis 15*(3), 233–254.

Cohen, D. (1995). What standards for national standards? *Phi Delta Kappan, 76*(10), 751–757.

Cohen, D. K. (1991). Revolution in one classroom. In S. Fuhrman & B. Malen (Eds.), *The politics of curriculum and testing* (pp. 102–123). London: Falmer Press.

Cohen, D. K., & Spillane, J. P. (1993). Policy and practice: The relations between governance and instruction. In S. H. Fuhrman (Ed.), *Designing coherent education policy* (pp. 35–95). San Francisco: Jossey-Bass.

Cohen, S. S. (1993). Geo-economics: Lessons from America's mistakes. In M. Carnoy, M. Castells, S. S. Cohen, & F. H. Cardoso (Eds.), *The new global economy in the information age* (pp. 97–147). University Park, PA: Pennsylvania State University Press.

Coleman, J., Hoffer, T., & Kilgore, S. (1982). *High school achievement: Public, Catholic and other private schools compared.* New York: Basic Books.

Cookson, P. W., Jr. (1995). Goals 2000: Framework for the new educational federalism. *Teachers College Record, 93*(3), 405–417.

Crystal, G. S. (1991). *In search of excess: The overcompensation of American executives.* New York: Norton.

Cubberley, E. P. (1909). *Changing conceptions of education.* Boston: Houghton Mifflin.

Cuthbertson, M. E. (1994). Governor Romer calls for expanded recycling. *eco-cycle times, 18,* 1.

Dahl, R. A. (1956). *A preface to democratic theory.* Chicago: University of Chicago Press.

Danziger S., & Gottschalk, P. (1985). The poverty of losing ground. *Challenge, 3,* 32–38.

Defense technology. (1995, June 10–16). *Economist, 335*(7918), 1–20.

DeMott, B. (1990). *The imperial middle.* New York: William Morrow.

DeParle, J. (1994, March 30). Clinton wages a quiet but energetic war against poverty. *New York Times,* p. A12.

DiIulio, J. J., Jr. (1995). Works better and costs less? Sweet and sour perspectives on the NPR. In D. F. Kettl & J. DiIulio (Eds.), *Inside the reinvention machine* (pp. 1–6). Washington, DC: Brookings Institution.

Edelman, M. (1964). *The symbolic uses of politics.* Urbana: University of Illinois Press.

Edelman, M. (1988). *Constructing the political spectacle.* Chicago: University of Chicago Press.

Edsall, T. B., & Edsall, M. D. (1991). *Chain reaction: The impact of race, rights, and taxes on American politics.* New York: Norton.

Educational Commission of the States. (1993). *How much are schools spending?* Denver: Educational Commission of the States.

Educational Testing Service. (1985). *The reading report card: Progress toward excellence in our schools. Trends in reading over four National Assessments, 1971–1984.* Princeton, NJ: National Assessment of Educational Progress, Educational Testing Service.

Educational Testing Service. (1990a). *The education reform decade.* Princeton, NJ: Educational Testing Service.

Educational Testing Service. (1990b). *The reading report card: 1971–88.* Princeton, NJ: National Assessment of Educational Progress, Educational Testing Service.

Educational Testing Service. (1991). *Trends in academic progress: Achievement of US students in science 1970 to 1990: mathematics 1973 to 1990: reading 1971 to 1990: and writing 1984 to 1990.* Washington, DC: U.S. Government Printing Office.

Ehrenreich, B. (1990). *Fear of falling: The inner life of the middle class.* New York: Harper.

Elliott, J. (1980). Implications of classroom research for professional development. In E. Hoyle & J. Megasry (Eds.), *World yearbook of education* (p. 25). London: Kogan Page.

Elliott, J. (1988). *Teachers as researchers: Implications for supervision and teacher education.* Paper delivered at the American Educational Research Association, New Orleans.

Ellwein, M. C., Glass, G. V., & Smith, M. L. (1988). Standards of competence: Propositions on the nature of testing reforms. *Educational Researcher, 17,* 4–9.

Elmore, R. F. (1993). The role of local school districts in instructional implementation. In S. H. Fuhrman (Ed.), *Designing coherent education policy* (pp. 96–124). San Francisco: Jossey-Bass.

Elmore, R. F., & Fuhrman, S. H. (1995). Opportunity to learn standards and the state role in education. *Teachers College Record, 93*(3), 432–457.

Elmore, R. F., & McLaughlin, M. W. (1988). *Steady work: Policy, practice and the reform of American education.* Santa Monica, CA: Rand Corporation.

Eraut, M. (1989). Teacher appraisal and/or teacher development: Friends or foe? In H. Simons & J. Elliott (Eds.), *Rethinking appraisal and assessment* (pp. 20–23). Buckingham, UK: Open University Press.

Expert Panel for Review of Federal Education Programs. (1993). *The federal investment in science, mathematics, engineering, and technology education: Where now? What next?* Washington, DC: National Science Foundation, Federal Coordinating Council on Science, Engineering, and Technology.

Ferris, J. M. (1992). School-based decision making: A principal-agent perspective. *Educational Evaluation and Policy Analysis, 14*(4), 333–346.

Firestone, W. A., Fuhrman, S. H., & Kirst, M. W. (1989). *The progress of reform: An appraisal of state education initiatives.* New Brunswick, NJ: Rutgers University.

*Forbes Magazine.* (1986, December 29). Are we spending too much on education? pp. 72–76.

Foreman, C. H. (1995). Reinventing politics? The NPR meets Congress. In D. F. Kettl & J. Dilulio (Eds.), *Inside the reinvention machine* (pp. 152–168). Washington, DC: Brookings Institution.

Fuhrman, S. H., & Massell, D. (1992). *Issues and strategies in systemic reform.* Mimeo, Consortium for Policy Research in Education, Rutgers.

Fullan, M. (1982). *The meaning of educational change.* New York: Teachers College Press.

Fullan, M. G., & Stiegelbauer, S. (1991). *The new meaning of educational change.* New York: Teachers College Press.

Galbraith, J. K. (1957). *The affluent society.* Boston: Houghton Mifflin.

Garcia, E. E., & Gonzalez, R. (1995). Issues in systemic reform for culturally and linguistically diverse students. *Teachers College Record, 93*(3), 418–431.

Garvey, G. (1995). False promises: The NPR in historical perspective. In D. F. Kettl & J. Dilulio (Eds.), *Inside the reinvention machine* (pp. 87–106). Washington, DC: Brookings Institution.

Gellner, E. (1983). *Nations and nationalism.* Oxford, UK: Basil Blackwell.

General Accounting Office. (1988). *R & D funding: The department of education in perspective.* Washington, DC: Government Printing Office. (GAO/PEMD-88-18FS).

General Accounting Office. (1993). *Educational achievement standards: NAGB's approach yields misleading interpretations.* Washington, DC: Government Printing Office. (GAO/PEMD-93-12).

Gilligan, C. (1982). *In a different voice.* Cambridge: Harvard University Press.

Gilpin, R. (1987). *The political economy of international relations.* Princeton, NJ: Princeton University Press.

Gintis, H. (1994). The political economy of school choice. *Teachers' College Record, 93*(3), 492–511.

Gipps, C. V. (1993, February). Large scale performance assessment: Lessons from the UK. Paper presented at School of Education, University of Colorado, Boulder.

Glass, G. V., & Ellwein, M. C. (1986). Reform by raising test standards. *Evaluation Comment* (pp. 1–6). Los Angeles: Center for the Study of Evaluation.

Glass, G. V., & Matthews, D. A. (1991). Are data enough? *Educational Researcher, 20*(3), 24–26.

Golding, E. B., & Rallis, S. F. (1993). *Principals of dynamic schools.* Newbury Park, CA: Corwin Press.

Good, T. L., & Mulryan, C. (1990). Teacher ratings: A call for teacher control and self-evaluation. In J. Millman & L. Darling-Hammond (Eds.), *The new handbook of teacher evaluation* (pp. 191–215). Newbury Park, CA: Sage Publications.

Goodlad, J. L. (1984). *A place called school.* New York: McGraw-Hill.

Gore, A. (1993). *Creating a government that works better and costs less: The report of the National Performance Review.* New York: Plume Books.

Greenstein, R. (1985). Losing faith in "Losing Ground." *The New Republic 3*(662), 12–17.

Guthrie, J. W. (1990). The evolving political economy of education and the implications for educational evaluation. *Educational Review, 42*(2), 109–131.

Hanushek, E. A. (1994). *Making schools work: Improving performance and controlling costs.* Washington, DC: Brookings Institution.

Harden, I. (1992). *The contracting state.* Buckingham UK: Open University Press.

Hayek, F. (1937). Economics and knowledge. *Economica,* 4, 33–54.

Heap, S. H., Hollis, M., Lyons, B., Sugden, R., & Weale, A. (1992). *The theory of choice: A critical guide.* Oxford, UK: Blackwell.

Hedges, L. V., Laine, R. D., & Greenwald, R. (1994). Does money matter? A meta-analysis of studies of the effects of differential school inputs on school outcomes. *Educational Researcher, 23,* 5–14.

Heilbroner, R. (1993). *21st century capitalism.* New York: W. W. Norton.

Hirsch, E. D., Jr. (1987). *Cultural literacy: What every American needs to know.* Boston: Houghton Mifflin.

Hirsch, F. (1982). Social limits to growth. In B. Barry & R. Hardin (Eds.), *Rational man and irrational society?* (pp. 158–170). Beverly Hills, CA: Sage Publications.

Hoggett, P. (1991). A new management in the public sector? *Policy and Politics, 19*(4), 243–256.

Hollenbeck, K. (1993). *Classrooms in the workplace.* Kalamazoo, MI: W. E. Upjohn Institute for Employment Research.

Holly, M. L. (1989). Perspective on teacher appraisal and teacher development. In H. Simons & J. Elliott (Eds.), *Rethinking appraisal and assessment* (pp. 100–118). Buckingham, UK: Open University Press.

House, E. R. (1974). *The politics of educational innovation.* Berkeley, CA: McCutchan Publishing.

House, E. R. (1981). Three Perspectives on Innovation: Technological, Political and Cultural. In R. Lehming and M. Kane (Eds.), *Improving schools: Using what we know.* (pp. 17–41). Beverly Hills: Sage Publications.

House, E. R. (1985). Undisciplined social science. *Evaluation News, 6*(2), 28–31.

House, E. R. (1988). *Jesse Jackson and the politics of charisma: The rise and fall of the PUSH/Excel program.* Boulder, CO: Westview Press.

House, E. R., Haug, C., & Norris, N. (1996). Producing evaluations in large bureaucracies. *Evaluation, 2*(2), 135–150.

House, E. R., & Lapan, S. D. (1988). The driver of the classroom: The teacher and school improvement. In R. Haskins & D. Macrae (Eds.), *Policies for America's public schools* (pp. 70–86). Norwood, NJ: Ablex Publishing.

House, E. R., Lapan, S., & Mathison, S. D. (1989). Teacher inference. *Cambridge Journal of Education, 19*(1), 53–58.

House, E. R., & Linn, R. L. (1987). Book review: *Losing Ground. Educational Evaluation and Policy Analysis, 8*(3), 324–328.

House, E. R., Linn, R., & Raths, J. (1982). Reports on New York City's Promotional Gates program. New York: Office of Educational Evaluation, New York City Public Schools.

House, E. R., & Madura, W. (1988). Race, gender, and jobs: *Losing Ground* on employment. *Policy Sciences, 21*, 351–382.

House, E. R., Mathison, S., & McTaggart, R. (1989). Validity and teacher inference. *Educational Researcher, 18*(7), 11–15.

House, E. R., & McQuillan, P. (1997). Perspectives on innovation. In A. Lieberman, M. Fullan, A. Hargreaves, & D. Hopkins (Eds.), *Roots of Change: International Handbook of Educational Change* (Vol. 1). Dordecht, The Netherlands: Kluwer.

House, E. R., Rivers, W., & Stufflebeam, D. L. (1974). An assessment of the Michigan accountability system. *Phi Delta Kappan, 55*(10), 663–669.

Howe, K. R. (1997). *Educational oppurtunities worth wanting: A contemporary theory of democracy, justice, and schooling.* New York: Teachers College Press.

Hume, E. (1985, September 17). A book attacking welfare system stirs furor in Washington. *The Wall Street Journal,* 1.

Hurley, S. L. (1989). *Natural reasons.* Oxford, UK: Oxford University Press.

Iannaccone, L., & Lutz, F. W. (1994). The crucible of democracy: The local arena. *Journal of Education Policy, 9*(5 & 6), 39–52.

Inequality. (1994). *Economist, 333*(7888), 19–21.

Investing in people. (1994, March 26). *Economist, 330*(7856), 85–86.

Johnson, D. (1988, July 13). Parents in Chicago to control schools under plan. *New York Times,* B6.

Johnson, S. M. (1990). *Teachers at work.* New York: Basic Books.

Kearns, D. (1976). *LBJ and the American dream.* New York: Harper and Row.

Kelsey, J. (1995). *The New Zealand experiment.* Auckland, NZ: Auckland University Press.

Kennedy, P. (1987). *The rise and fall of the great powers.* New York: Random House.

Kennedy, P. (1993). *Preparing for the twenty-first century.* New York: Random House.

Kettl, D. F. (1993). *Sharing power: Public governance and private markets.* Washington, DC: Brookings Institution.

Kettl, D. F. (1994). *Reinventing government? Appraising the National Performance Review.* Washington, DC: Brookings Institution.

Kettl, D. F. (1995). Building lasting reform: Enduring questions, missing answers. In D. F.

Kettl & J. Dilulio (Eds.), *Inside the reinvention machine* (pp. 9–83). Washington, DC: Brookings Institution.

Kingdon, J. W. (1984). *Agendas, alternatives, and public policies.* New York: Harper Collins.

Kirst, M. (1990). A review of J. E. Chubb and T. M. Moe, *Politics, markets, and American schools. Politics of Education Bulletin, 17*(1), 2–3.

Kogan, M. (1986). *Education accountability.* London: Hutchinson.

Kogan, M., & Kogan, D. (1983). *The attack on higher education.* London: Kogan Page.

Kohlberg, L. (1969). The cognitive developmental approach to socialization. In D. A. Goslin (Ed.), *Handbook of socialization theory and research* (pp. 369–389). Chicago: Rand McNally.

Koretz, D. M., Madaus, G. E., Haertal, E., & Beaton, A. (1992). *National educational standards and testing: A response to the recommendations of the National Council on Education Standards and Testing.* Santa Monica, CA: Rand Corporation.

Kozol, J. (1991). *Savage inequalities.* New York: Crown Publishers.

Kristol, I. (1972). *On the democratic idea in America.* New York: Harper & Row.

Krugman, P. (1992). *The age of diminished expectations: US Economic policy in the 1990s.* Cambridge, MA: MIT Press.

Krugman, P. (1994a). Competitiveness: A dangerous obsession. *Foreign Affairs, 73*(2), 28–44.

Krugman, P. (1994b). *Peddling prosperity.* New York: Norton.

Lapan, S. D., & Hays, P. A. (1992). Developing special programs for minority gifted youth: Northern Arizona University's teacher training program. *Potential, 18*(7), 1–3.

Lasch, C. (1995). *The revolt of the elites.* New York: W. W. Norton.

Lasswell, H. (1971). *A preview of the policy sciences.* New York: American Elsevier.

Levin, H. M. (1993a). Education and jobs: A proactive view. 7th Annual International Research-Practice Conference on Education and Work. Ontario Institute for Studies of Education, Toronto.

Levin, H. M. (1993b). The economics of education for at-risk students. In E. P. Hoffman (Ed.), *Essays on the economics of education* (pp. 11–33). Kalamazoo, MI: W. E. Upjohn Institute for Employment Research.

Levy, F. (1987a, May 3). Actually, we are all getting poorer. *New York Times,* p. 2F.

Levy, F. (1987b). *Dollars and dreams: The changing American income distribution.* New York: Russell Sage Foundation.

Linn, R. L., & Dunbar, S. B. (1990). The nation's report card goes home: Good news and bad about trends in achievement. *Phi Delta Kappan, 72*(2), 127–133.

Liston, D. (1988). *Capitalist schools.* New York: Routledge.

Little, D. (1991). *Varieties of social explanation.* Boulder, CO: Westview Press.

Lortie, D. (1975). *School teacher: A sociological study.* Chicago: University of Chicago Press.

Macpherson, C. B. (1973). *Democratic theory.* Oxford, UK: Oxford University Press.

Macpherson, C. B. (1977). *The life and times of liberal democracy.* Oxford, UK: Oxford University Press.

Macpherson, C. B. (1987). *The rise and fall of economic justice.* Oxford, UK: Oxford University Press.

Madura, W. (1990). *Black educational achievement and the educational underclass.* Unpublished dissertation, University of Colorado, Boulder, CO.

Malen, B. (1994). The micropolitics of education: Mapping the multiple dimensions of power relations in school politics. *Journal of Education Policy, 9*(5&6), 147–167.

Manegold, C. S. (1994, February 9). 2 bills to bolster school methods clear the Senate. *New York Times*, p. A4.

Marquand, D. (1988). *The principled society.* London: Fontana.

Massy, W. F., & Wilger, A. K. (1992). Productivity in postsecondary education. *Educational Evaluation and Policy Analysis, 14*(4), 361–376.

Mazzoni, T. L. (1994). State policy making and school reform: Influences and influentials. *Journal of Education Policy, 9*(5&6), 53–73.

McCloskey, D. N. (1990). *If you're so smart: The narrative of economic expertise.* Chicago: University of Chicago Press.

McDougall, W. A. (1995). Whose history? Whose standards? *Commentary, 99*(5), 36–43.

McLaughlin, M. W., & Talbert, J. E. (1993). How the world of students and teachers challenges policy coherence. In S. H. Fuhrman (Ed.), *Designing coherent education policy* (pp. 220–249). San Francisco: Jossey-Bass.

McNeil, L. M. (1986). *Contradictions of control.* New York: Routledge.

McTaggart, R. (1985). *Conditions for action research.* Unpublished doctoral thesis, University of Illinois, Champaign-Urbana.

Meier, D. (1995). *The power of their ideas.* Boston: Beacon Press.

Meyer, R. H. (1993). Can schools be held accountable for good performance? In E. P. Hoffman (Ed.), *Essays on the economics of education* (pp. 75–109). Kalamazoo, MI: W. E. Upjohn Institute for Employment Research.

Mohrman, S. A., Lawler, E. E., & Mohrman, A. M. (1992). Applying employee involvement in schools. *Educational Evaluation and Policy Analysis, 14*(4), 347–360.

Monk, D. H. (1992). Education productivity research: An update and assessment of its role in education finance reform. *Educational Evaluation and Policy Analysis, 14*(4), 307–332.

Muncey, D. E., & McQuillan, P. J. (1993a). Preliminary findings from a five-year study of the Coalition of Essential Schools. *Phi Delta Kappan, 6,* 37–45.

Muncey, D. E., & McQuillan, P. J. (1993b). Education reform as revitalization movement. *American Journal of Education, 101*(4), 393–431.

Murray, C. (1984). *Losing ground: American social policy 1950–1980.* New York: Basic Books.

Nasar S. (1992, March 5). The 1980s: A very good time for the very rich. *New York Times,* p. 1.

National Center for Educational Statistics. (1990). *Federal support for education: Fiscal years 1980 to 1989* (NCES 90-662). Washington, DC: U.S. Department of Education.

National Education Goals Panel. (1994). *National education goals report: Building a nation of learners.* Washington, DC: U.S. Government Printing Office.

North Central Regional Educational Laboratory. (1992). *Monitoring implementation of the Chicago public schools' systemwide school reform goals and objectives plan.* Oak Brook, IL: North Central Regional Educational Laboratory.

O'Day, J. A., & Smith, M. S. (1993). Systemic reform and educational opportunity. In S. H. Fuhrman (Ed.), *Designing coherent education policy* (pp. 250–312). San Francisco: Jossey-Bass.

Odden, A. (1989). School funding changes: 1960 to 1988. Los Angeles: University of Southern California.

Odden, A. (1992). Discovering educational productivity: An organizational approach. *Educational Evaluation and Policy Analysis, 14*(4), 303–305.

Odden, A., & Massy, W. (1992). *Funding schools and universities: Improving productivity and equity.*

New Brunswick, NJ: Consortium for Policy Research in Education, Rutgers University. (RR-026).

Odden, A. R. (Ed.). (1991). *Education policy implementation.* Albany: State University of New York Press.

Office of Educational Evaluation, New York City Public Schools. (1982). *A final evaluation of the 1981–1982 promotional gates program.* Brooklyn, NY: New York City Schools.

Osborne, D., & Gaebler, T. (1992). *Reinventing government.* Reading, MA: Addison-Wesley.

Peterson, P. (1994). Foreword to the study of education politics. *Journal of Education Policy, 9*(5&6), xiv.

Phillips, K. (1990). *The politics of the rich and poor.* New York: Random House.

Phillips, K. (1993). *Boiling point: Democrats, Republicans, and the decline of middle-class prosperity.* New York: Random House.

Polanyi, M. (1962). *Personal knowledge.* New York: Harper and Row.

Pollit, C. (1990). Performance indicators, root and branch. In M. Cave, M. Kogan, & R. Smith (Eds.), *Output and performance measurement in government* (pp. 167–178). London: Jessica Kingsley Publishers.

Porter, A. C. (1990). Assessing national goals: Some measurement dilemmas. In *The assessment of national educational goals. Proceedings of the 1990 Educational Testing Service Invitational Conference* (pp. 25–35). Princeton, NJ: Educational Testing Service.

Pusey, M. (1991). *Economic rationalism in Canberra.* Cambridge, UK: Cambridge University Press.

Putterman, L. (Ed.). (1986). *The economic nature of the firm.* Cambridge, UK: Cambridge University Press.

Radin, B. A. (1995). Varieties of reinvention: Six NPR "success stories." In D. F. Kettl & J. Dilulio (Eds.), *Inside the reinvention machine* (pp. 107–130). Washington, DC: Brookings Institution.

Ravitch, D., & Finn, C. E., Jr. (1987). *What do our 17-year-olds know?* New York: Harper and Row.

Resnick, L., & Tucker, M. (1992). *The new standards project: 1992–1995. A proposal.* Pittsburgh: Learning Research and Development Center, University of Pittsburgh.

Riley, R. W. (1995). Reflections on goals 2000. *Teachers College Record, 93*(3), 380–388.

Rogge, W. M. (1967). The teacher is his own best change agent. *Accent On Talent, 1*(4), pp. 1, 4.

Rohatyn, F. (1990). The fall and rise of New York City. *The New York Review of Books, 37*(17), 40–44.

Rosenbaum, D. E. (1994, February 18). The Clinton difference? Not much in the budget. *New York Times,* p. 18.

Rowen, H. (1968). *The free enterprisers: Kennedy, Johnson, and the business establishment.* New York: Putnam.

Sarason, S. B. (1990). *The predictable failure of educational reform.* San Francisco: Jossey-Bass.

Schön, D. C. (1983). *The reflective practitioner.* New York: Basic Books.

Schumpeter, J. A. (1942). *Capitalism, socialism, and democracy* (3rd ed.). New York: Harper Colophon Books.

Scriven, M. (1985). Evaluation as a paradigm for educational research. In E. R. House (Ed.), *New directions for educational evaluation* (pp. 53–67). Lewes, England: Falmer Press.

Sen, A. (1987). *On ethics and economics.* Oxford, UK: Blackwell.

Shavelson, R. J., & Stern, P. (1981). Research on teachers' pedagogical thoughts, judgments, decisions, and behavior. *Review of Educational Research, 51*(47), 455–498.

Shepard, L. A., & Smith, M. L. (Eds.). (1989). *Flunking grades: Research and policies on retention.* London: Falmer Press.

Shields, P. M., Corcoran, T. B., & Zucker, A. A. (1994). *Evaluation of the National Science Foundation's Statewide Systemic Initiatives (SSI) program: First year report.* Menlo Park, CA: SRI International.

Silk, L. (1992, January 31). The basic conflict in budget policy. *New York Times,* p. C2.

Simon, H. (1961). *Administrative behavior.* New York: Macmillan.

Smith, M. L., Noble, A. J., Haag, S., Seck, M., & Taylor, K. (1994). *The consequences of measurement-driven reform: Survey of Arizona educators.* Phoenix: Arizona State University, Southwest Educational Policy Studies.

Smith, M. S. (1995). Education reform in America's public schools: The Clinton agenda. In D. Ravitch (Ed.), *Debating the future of American education: Do we need national standards and assessments?* (pp. 9–32). Washington, DC: Brookings Institution.

Smith, M. S., & O'Day, J. (1991). Systemic school reform. In S. H. Fuhrman & B. Malen (Eds.), *The politics of curriculum and testing* (pp. 233–267). London: Falmer Press.

Smith, M. S., & Scoll, B. W. (1995). The Clinton human capital agenda. *Teachers College Record, 93*(3), 389–404.

Songer, N. B. (1995). Can technology bring students closer to science? In K. Tobin & B. Fraser (Eds.), *The International Handbook of Science* (pp. 87–105). The Netherlands: Kluwer.

Songer, N. B. (1996). Knowledge construction through global exchange and dialogue: A case of kids as global scientists. *The Journal of Learning Sciences, 3,* 53–72.

Sroufe, G. E. (1991). Uncertain future for education research despite increased congressional support. *Educational Researcher, 20*(1), 24–26.

Stake, R. E. (1985). An evolutionary view of program improvement. In E. R. House (Ed.), *New directions for educational evaluation* (pp. 89–102). Lewes, England: Falmer Press.

Stecher, B. M., & Klein, S. P. (1997). The cost of science performance assessments in large-scale testing programs. *Educational Evaluation and Policy Analysis, 19*(1), 1–14.

Steinberg, J. (1996, November 21). School budget study shows 43% is spent in classrooms. *New York Times,* p. B8.

Stevenson, D. L. (1995). Goals 2000 and local reform. *Teachers College Record, 93*(3), 458–466.

Stiglitz, J. E. (1994). *Whither socialism?* Cambridge, MA: MIT Press.

Thurow, L. (1992). *Head to head: The coming economic battle among Japan, Europe, and America.* New York: Morrow.

Tolchin, M. (1991, February 4). Cuts after decade of cuts: Governors grim at meeting. *New York Times,* C-2.

Tyack, D. B. (1974). *The one best system: A history of American urban education.* Cambridge: Harvard University Press.

Tyler, R. W. (1989). *Educational evaluation: Classic works of Ralph W. Tyler.* G. F. Madaus & D. Stufflebeam (Eds.). Boston: Kluwer Academic Publishers.

Tyler, R. W., Lapan, S. D., Moore, J. C., Rivers, L. W., & Skibo, D. B. (1978). *The Florida accountability program: An evaluation of its educational soundness and implementation.* Washington, DC: National Education Association.

U.S. Department of Education. (1986). *What works: Research about teaching and learning.*

U.S. Department of Education. (1991). *America 2000: An education strategy.* Washington, DC.

U.S. Department of Education. (1992). World class standards for American education.

Uchitelle, L. (1994, February 4). Male, educated and in a pay bind. *New York Times,* C-1.

Vaizey, J. (1962). *The economics of education.* New York: Free Press of Glencoe.

Wargo, M. J. (1994, November 3). *Impact of the president's reinvention plan on federal evaluation activity.* Paper delivered to American Evaluation Association, Boston.

Waslander, S., & Thrupp, M. (1995). Choice, competition, and segregation: An empirical analysis of a New Zealand secondary school market, 1990–1993. *Journal of Education Policy, 10*(1), 1–26.

Weiss, C., & Cambone, J. (1994). Principals, shared decision making, and school reform. *Educational Evaluation and Policy Analysis, 16*(3), 287–301.

Williamson, O. E. (1975). *Markets and hierarchies.* New York: Free Press.

Williamson, O. E. (1985). *The economic institutions of capitalism: Firms, markets, and relational contracting.* New York: Free Press.

Wilson, J. Q. (1989). *Bureaucracy.* New York: Basic Books.

Winerip, M. (1994a, February 3). Overhauling school grants: much debate but little gain. *New York Times,* p. A1.

Winerip, M. (1994b, February 3). Trying to manage federal aid, Education Dept. can't keep up. *New York Times,* p. A1.

Wirt, F. M., & Harman, G. (Eds.). (1986). *Education, recession, and the world village.* London: Falmer Press.

Wirt, F., & Kirst, M. (1982). *The politics of education: Schools in conflict.* Berkeley, CA: McCutchan.

Wirth, A. G. (1992). *Education and work for the year 2000.* San Francisco: Jossey-Bass.

Womack, J. P., Jones, D. T., & Roos, D. (1990). *The machine that changed the world: The story of lean production.* New York: Harper Perennial.

Wong, K. K. (1994). The politics of education: From political science to multidisciplinary inquiry. *Journal of Education Policy, 9*(5&6), 21–35.

Wong, K. K. (1995). Can the big-city school system be governed? In P. W. Cookson, Jr., & B. Schneider, (Eds.), *Transforming schools* (pp. 457–488). New York: Garland Publishing.

# INDEX

153

# ABOUT THE AUTHOR

Ernest R. House is a professor in the School of Education at the University of Colorado at Boulder. His primary interests are evaluation and policy. He has been a visiting scholar at UCLA, Harvard, New Mexico, and in England, Spain, Sweden, Austria, and Australia. Books include *The Politics of Educational Innovation, Survival in the Classroom* (with S. Lapan), *Evaluating with Validity: Jesse Jackson and the Politics of Charisma,* and *Professional Evaluation: Social Impact and Political Consequences.* He is recipient of the Harold E. Lasswell Prize for the article contributing the most to the theory and practice of the policy sciences in 1989 and of the Lazarsfeld Award for Evaluation Theory, presented by the American Evaluation Association in 1990.